SUSAN GUTTERIDGE

family MATTERS

HOW MR GINNS
MET MR GUTTERIDGE

SUSAN GUTTERIDGE

family
MATTERS

HOW MR GINNS
MET MR GUTTERIDGE

MEREO
Cirencester

Mereo Books

1A The Wool Market Dyer Street Cirencester Gloucestershire GL7 2PR
An imprint of Memoirs Publishing www.mereobooks.com

Family matters: 978-1-86151-379-3

First published in Great Britain in 2014
by Mereo Books, an imprint of Memoirs Publishing

The address for Memoirs Publishing Group Limited can be found at
www.memoirspublishing.com

The Memoirs Publishing Group Ltd Reg. No. 7834348

The Memoirs Publishing Group supports both The Forest Stewardship Council® (FSC®) and
the PEFC® leading international forest-certification organisations. Our books carrying both the
FSC label and the PEFC® and are printed on FSC®-certified paper. FSC® is the only
forest-certification scheme supported by the leading environmental organisations including
Greenpeace. Our paper procurement policy can be found at
www.memoirspublishing.com/environment

Typeset in 11/16pt Bembo
by Wiltshire Associates Publisher Services Ltd. Printed and bound in Great Britain by
Printondemand-Worldwide, Peterborough PE2 6XD

ACKNOWLEDGEMENTS

I would like to thank Alex Sherwin, Julia Cox and
Steph Glen, also my husband David Barlow, my son
James Hadfield and my daughter Cassie Greenwood, for
their help and encouragement in getting this book published.

CHAPTER ONE

"It's a beautiful girl, Mr Ginns, do come and see, she's lovely."
Frank Ginns had been dispatched downstairs after wishing his
wife good luck. He had left the two women to do whatever
women had to do during a birth.

Frank felt anxious and lonely; he wanted a drink to calm his
nerves, but it was dark and everywhere would be closed now.
Then he remembered the cooking sherry in the kitchen.
Grabbing a candle, he went through to the kitchen to the
newly-bought cupboard, took a glass from the draining board,
filled it and drank it all without a thought.

Suddenly he heard a faint call from upstairs, and he climbed
the stairs two at a time. He burst into the bedroom to see his
new daughter. They'd discussed names before Florence became
pregnant, one day while visiting Hathern, near Loughborough,
where Florence's grandparents lived. They had chosen Frank for
a boy and Ann for a girl, so Ann it was.

Ann was so small, lying there wrapped up in a shawl knitted
by Mrs Kilby. It was her first day, August 18 1906. It still was not
light, though dawn had broken. The two "midwives" looked

weary but satisfied, proud even. Florence lay proudly cuddling the baby, tired but happy. She looked over at the two who had been with her throughout the night.

"Thank you both so much, and also please thank Walter and Jack for looking after your boys Ellen, and Jack for not making a fuss when you rushed out. You didn't even have time to replait your hair, either of you!"

After they'd left there was a lonely silence in the room. It reminded Florence of coming home after a wedding. She shook herself out of her despondency, looked at Ann and decided to put her in an old but sturdy wooden drawer which she'd readied before the birth. Frank hadn't been around much then – and where was he now? The pubs weren't open yet. She guessed that the cooking sherry bottle was empty.

It was silent apart from the sound of a few horses in Highcross Street. Slowly, ever so slowly, Leicester was waking to a cloudless sky. Florence drifted off to sleep, only to be awoken by Frank, who had been over the road to Mrs Cashubar's for some Woodbines and sherry.

Frank stiffened when she asked him if he would ride over to Belgrave to tell both their families the news of Ann's arrival. Frank said he had a lot to do now that the station was well on its way, construction wise. Ann's birth had been put to one side; she was only a day old.

Frank woke early; Florence still slept, as did Ann, judging by the noises coming from the drawer. Hell, it was cold. Glancing at the fireplace, he saw the ash had tumbled out, leaving cold and blackened wood where Florence had banked it up there. Frank dressed quickly, taking his collar-studs down with him.

It was warmer downstairs. Frank thought to himself that Charlie Hancock must have arrived early and begun his day's work. Frank had only employed Charlie a few days before; he had been a groom. Frank's friends knew him and said what a conscientious worker he was. He'd been working for the Glovers in Birstall until Frank had offered him work. His job would be to light the fires, clean the shoes and open the doors to Highcross Street. Charlie was a short man, about the same age as Frank and originally from Bristol; he had kept his dialect.

The previous day had been wasted going to Belgrave, where he had met some men in the Hat & Beaver who might be useful with regard to the Great Central station. He usually used the Joiner's Arms, which was only over the road from his new home.

Frank walked to the white Belfast sink in the kitchen, where he looked at himself in old piece of mirror before he washed last night away from his eyes and his face. He had so much to do today. One thing he must get sorted was the plans for the entrance between Highcross Street and the stables; his father was coming on Sunday and it would be good to have something to show him, especially as he would be paying!

He thought of Harrison's, the builders, next to the church. The church – oh, Florence could sort the christening out.

Frank was about to put his collar on when Florence appeared with Ann.

"Morning, Frank" she said. "I must have been woken up by Ann, or the cold - why was it so cold? It's warmer down here, I should have fed her here."

"Morning Florence. I was up early. I have a lot to do today, I shall be glad when things get back to normal. I'm going to the

Harrison's this morning to see if they'll give us a quote for doing the front of the two houses so we can get carriages down to the stables. What are you doing today?"

"I must go to All Saints and book Ann's christening as Harrison's are very close. Will you walk down with me? I am very excited to use the new pram my parents gave us, aren't you? We'll go when we've had something to eat. Porridge maybe, it's so cold!" she said jokingly. Frank didn't smile.

They arrived at Jack Harrison's, the builder, first. Frank knew his father would need three quotes, but at least he would have something to show him on Sunday. Frank and Florence parted at the gateway to Harrison's, leaving Frank to walk down to the yard to the office.

Florence felt slightly nervous; though she had been to church many times before, she had never been to All Saints. It was Tuesday morning and she doubted anyone was be in there.

Florence kissed Frank farewell and turned with the new pram down the slope to All Saints church. It was hard to miss, as it protruded out into the pavement. She stood and looked at the unusual clock, said to have been built by one of the congregation. Fixed about 18 feet above the main door into the church, it was a black painted rectangle with a round clock face in the top half with gold Roman numerals and golden hands. On the piece nearest the door were two golden male figures about 12 inches tall with sticks, with which they struck the bell every hour.

Florence didn't understand why she felt nervous and breathless; she'd been into churches plenty of times before. She decided to carry Ann and leave the pram behind the bushes. Putting her hand on the heavy metal doorknob, she opened the door gingerly. On a Tuesday morning there wouldn't be anyone around, surely. She showed Ann the font where in a few days she would be christened, then walked down the aisle, talking to the baby as she walked. She saw the motes of dust lit by the shafts of sunlight coming through the windows, and told her they were baby fairies who would grow at the same time as she would.

She was shocked to see that there was a man kneeling by the altar. He stared up at her, as surprised as she was. He stood up and she saw that he was wearing a baize apron; a cleaner, she thought.

"Good morning, my name is William Gutteridge" he said. "I'm one of the churchwardens here, may I help you?"

"Er, good morning, I am Mrs Ginns" replied Florence. "My husband and I recently moved to Highcross Street from Belgrave, and a few days after that I gave birth to Ann here. The main reason I am here is to see the Reverend Swingler about her christening."

"I'm so sorry, the Reverend is away in Thurlaston" replied Mr Gutteridge. "He left yesterday. But let me take your details."

He asked for her name and address, the name of her husband, if Ann was to have any more names, who were going to be the three godparents and what relationship they had with Ann. He wrote it all down in a big book he'd fetched from the vestry.

"When would you like it to be?" he asked.

"We would like it to be at three o'clock on a Sunday" she said. "We will be asking guests from as far away as Hathern."

William looked at Florence in a new light. He liked a woman who was confident and could speak her mind.

Florence was lying in bed, on her back. It was dark, and there were lights left on in Highcross Street. The pains were encompassing her belly more and more frequently. It was no good, she would have to wake Frank. Her screams finally penetrated his sleep.

"Frank, you must go and get help" she said. "The baby is coming. Fetch Mrs Disley or Mrs Johnson, anyone from Friars Causeway. Now!"

Florence was in agony and the pain was worse after each contraction. She needed a gin and hot water. She told Frank to go and get help. She wanted her mother, who had given her gin for period pains, but she was in Belgrave, with her husband and son, Francis, all calmly asleep without a care of what was happening on the other side of Leicester.

Florence and Frank had not long ago moved to Highcross Street. They had married at St Philip's Church on Belgrave Road and decided to look for premises nearer to the long-awaited Great Central Railway station. Frank and his father were horse sellers and carriers and Frank had met Florence at the Dolphin, the public house where Florence had been born.

Her parents had been very unsure about Frank as he grew up. He liked a drink and went into the Dolphin most nights. Florence's parents often looked on with mild amusement, noting that he and Florence seemed to be getting closer and closer. The only time they disliked him was when he was in with his shooting friends, all of whom were considerably older than he was and had more money to spend. Sometimes it really was 'booze in, brass out' with him, but he was fond of Florence and she of him. He had a good eye when choosing a horse, worked hard for his father and looked as if he had a good future ahead of him as a cabbie.

Frank awoke with a terrible headache. it took him long, bleary minutes to realise that he was in his new home and no longer in Loughborough Road.

Florence called again. "Go and get help, the baby is coming, go now!"

Frank was dressing as she shouted. "I'm going!" he said. Florence could hear him thundering down the stairs, but she was screaming and crying too much to hear much else.

After what seemed an eternity, Florence heard a scuffle from below. Frank was back with Mrs Disley and young Annie Johnson, recently married but willing to do whatever she could to help. Ellen Disley was a short, busty lady who already had four boys. She bustled into the darkened room, telling Annie to get more lights on. She could see there wasn't long to go and told Annie to get a cold towel and to talk to her, keeping an eye on her breathing.

Mrs Disley and Annie lived in two of the four small cottages; their gardens abutted the stables in the same premises. Annie lived at number 1, Ellen at number 3. Ellen was in her forties, while Annie was young enough to do what Ellie told her; a good pair.

Frank's father had been with Frank to look for premises before. The station was ready and they needed somewhere with stables for about four horses, harnesses, carriages, a hansom cab and a house for a family.

They looked at Churchgate, though they were pipped to the post by John White. They looked on Highcross Street at Earps', the funeral directors, but Earp didn't want a partner. They finally looked at the one which was the nearest to the station and obviously more expensive. There was a back way through to Great Central Street but the four cottages were there. Sam, Frank's father, thought they'd found the perfect position and said he would help them buy it and the four cottages as well.

Florence thought she must get Frank to ride over to Belgrave with her. She wasn't taking Ann out before she had been seen by Dr Angus, whose surgery was only 100 yards up Highcross Street, on the other side. She was surprised at Frank's reluctance to go. The Cambers were in Belgrave too and would be excited to meet Ann. Florence had arranged for Mrs Disley to come round to help with Ann, but knew it would be too much for her with four boys and was wondering if maybe Annie, young as she was, might like to be employed full time to help with Ann and to keep the house.

When Frank was back from Belgrave they had to register the birth and get Frank to go to All Saints and arrange the christening. Soon she would be back to normal.

CHAPTER TWO

"Where have you been?" snapped Florence. "You stink of cigarettes and booze! I know it takes a while to ride to Belgrave, but you've been so long!"

"First I went to see my parents" replied Frank. "They were so happy. Then I went across the yard to tell Francis, who was in the stables, about to take two of the horses to be reshod in the village. He was excited too. An uncle! I told them they were invited to Highcross Street to eat with us on Sunday, and to see Ann for the first time. Then I went to The Dolphin sand repeated it all again. They will be coming too, probably all in one of my father's carriages." He omitted to mention the two hours he'd spent in the Hat & Beaver.

Frank undressed and was soon snoring beside her. Once Ann had been fed Florence took her back into the drawer, stoked the fire, turned the gas off, said her prayers and went to sleep.

"I have just begun the veg for tomorrow. Glad you're up and almost dressed. I think Annie Johnson will be here very soon for her interview, so you can see if you think she will be good to look after Ann and clean and do a bit of shopping and cooking. I may well see if she can help me prepare tomorrow's dinner."

"I liked what I saw of the girl, how old do you think she is?"

"I think she's in her early twenties, but we'll know more soon."

Florence dried her hands and looked at the clock. At the same time there was a knock at the door.

"Now you're washed and dressed, will you go and show her into the sitting room? I'll make some tea and bring it in."

A few minutes later Florence went in with a heavily-laden tray.

"Hello Annie, thank you for being so prompt, you came by Highcross Street. I'm sorry, I forgot to ask Mr Ginns to unlock the door through the stables."

"Good morning Mrs Ginns, you are looking much better, how is Ann? And how are you? A week tonight, seems to have gone by very quickly."

"It does indeed. Would you like tea and a biscuit?"

"Yes please."

"My wife and I are wondering if you would like to come to work for us, Annie" said Frank. "To help Florence with Ann and also help with the house, shopping and cooking, in fact it would be good if you could stay on. We have a family party tomorrow and Florence could do with some help with and cooking, couldn't you dear?"

"I would love to look after Ann and be your housekeeper" she said. "How much will you be paying?"

"I think we can pay you two pounds per week."

"Well, I would like to talk it over with Jack first. I can come round tomorrow to help you, but I have plans for today, I'm afraid. Oh, Jack would be happy to make a bigger cradle for Ann. Could you ask Mr Cambers for some wood please?"

Florence had forgotten that Annie would know that her father was supplying Mr Ginns with wood; they were going into partnership. Then she remembered that he had a put up a sign outside, which Florence had thought was going to be pulled down when Mr Harrison began to alter the front of number 98. Frank had seen two others but decided on Jack (another Jack) Harrison, as he had put in the best quote and lived nearby.

The church bells had stopped, and Florence hoped the vicar had returned from Thurlaston; soon Rev Swingler would call to see them. She remembered that Frank must go to Pocklington's Walk to register Ann's birth. It was 12th August, 1906.

Annie picked up her gloves. "Thank you for the tea and the offer of a job" she said. "I'm sure Jack will agree to your terms. I will go and see him before I see you about half past eight tomorrow."

"I'll let you out the stable door way, Mrs Johnson, I'll leave it unlocked until tomorrow."

When Annie had left, Florence carried the tray into the kitchen and began to wash the teacups. There was a knock at the front door.

"Will you get it, Frank?" she said. "My hands are wet and I've my apron, I was just about to make the batter for the Yorkshires."

"It drives me insane when people arrive unannounced" said Frank.

"Me too, I have my day all planned."

Frank went to the door to see that the caller was Mr Gutteridge from the church.

"Good afternoon Mr Ginns" he said. "Your wife and I met at All Saints a few days ago, when she came to book Ann's christening. I told her that Rev. Swingler would call to see her on his return from Thurlaston. Is she in?"

"She is, busy preparing for a family visit tomorrow."

"Oh yes, she told me about it. It seems I held Ann before most."

"Did you really? Florence hasn't mentioned it."

"Yes, your wife looked tired, so I suggested she sat on a pew, and while she did I held Ann."

"Oh, she mentioned that. I'm sure she would like to see you, would you like a cup of tea?"

"I would, it seems a while since breakfast."

Florence's heart skipped a beat when she heard who the caller was. "I'll make some more tea then" she said. She thought she would never get the batter made. She took her apron off, thinking Ann needed feeding too.

Walking to the sitting room, she felt herself trembling with excitement, as well as embarrassment at the furniture, which was hand-me-downs from her parents, including the oval oak gateleg table which they would use tomorrow. She wondered where the tablecloths and best cutlery was. Annie would have to find it.

"Mr Gutteridge, good afternoon. Mr Swingler must be back, I heard the bells. We have not really talked about the christening, though I think I know the three godparents."

"I don't think you discussed it with me."

"I thought we would discuss it when Mr Swingler calls."

"Ah well, the Reverend asked me to tell you he would like to call at 11.30 on Tuesday. If that isn't convenient I'll be seeing him at the church tomorrow."

"That will be convenient for me" said Frank.

As Florence was about to speak, the sound of crying came from Ann's room.

"You'll have to excuse me, I must go up and feed her" she said. Why don't you two go and have a drink over the road? I shall be forty-five minutes. Please come back for lunch Mr Gutteridge, and bring Frank with you please, or he will be there until closing time."

" I know you need to go to Ann, but please call me William, and I would love to eat with you. Thank you."

Florence went up the back stairs, which was quicker but involved a large step up the first step. She never knew whether to change or feed Ann first, but this time it was obvious.

She sat on an old Lloyd Loom chair she had brought with her from Belgrave and fed Ann, who appeared to be very hungry. Then she changed her and went downstairs, just as the men walked in. Wondering what to do with Ann, she asked Frank to bring the pram.

While he was gone, William asked if he could hold Ann for a while. Florence was grateful that he cared enough. He and Frank were around the same age, she thought, but Frank had never shown any interest in Ann, which saddened her greatly.

Frank came in and asked what he should do with the pram, glancing at William with fascination. Why, he wondered, was he holding Ann?

"I'll put her outside whilst we eat" said Florence, taking Ann from William. When she returned, she left the men whilst she went into the kitchen to poach three eggs and make toast and tea. Then she went in to set the table. When she returned with a loaded tray, the men were talking about horses, a shared interest.

She'd put a drop of vinegar in with the eggs, a tip of her mother's. She was coming tomorrow! Panic swept through her. The toast was done and she buttered the three slices without thinking and put the meal together. She carried the three plates through and they all sat down to eat.

"William lives on St Nicholas Street Florence, did you know?" said Frank.

"Why don't you go to St. Nicholas, if you don't mind me asking, William?"

"I went there once, but I didn't like Rev. Gill at all, so I went to All Saints. I get on very well with Mr Swingler."

"Being newcomers we don't know anyone yet" said Frank. "We'll meet Rev Swingler on Tuesday you said, I must put it in my diary. We need to get it organised. My parents are coming tomorrow and we can talk to them about it. Where do you stable your horses, William?"

"Oh, just at the back of where I live, in Duns Lane, bit of a trek now the station's up and running but I keep two carts there too, and some men work for me there. I think I told you this though Frank, at the pub, didn't I?"

"Anyone like more tea?" said Florence.

"Thank you, but look at the time, I have things to do" said William. "As I'm sure you do, with your families coming over tomorrow."

"Call in any time you're passing" said Florence.

"We can always go for a drink over the road" Frank suggested, unsurprisingly. With that William left.

Both the Ginns were happy he'd called. Florence cleared the table and Frank sat in his favourite green winged chair, reading a brochure. Florence thought he'd be asleep before she'd finished in the kitchen, mentally making a note not to go upstairs to sleep after last time. At last once she had washed up and cleared up she could make the batter for the Yorkshires. She knew to use plain flour, to make it the night before (something to do with allowing the gluten to form, an old chef had told her mother years before) and to have your fat sizzling in the oven to get the puddings to rise. Also, as a Cambers family tradition, her mother used to sing, usually out of tune, whilst she beat it, lifting the fork high to be sure there was lots of air getting into the batter. Then Florence put it on the draining board for the night.

Now she had to go and sit looking at Frank. Perhaps he would tell her, in depth, what Jack Harrison was going to do to numbers 98 and 100 and when, and how much it was going to cost and where the money was coming from.

Frank was asleep, the brochure at his feet. She looked at him, studying his face; he was getting so yellow. Forget Mr Harrison, she must see that he went to see Dr Angus. Florence thought it was all to do with his drinking; he'd always liked a drop. She wondered how his shooting friends in Glooston ever managed to shoot any birds.

To take her mind off Frank, she returned to thinking about dinner tomorrow. She planned to get dressed about seven, and Annie said she would be there around 8.30. She hoped she would be prompt.

It was beginning to get dark and it was even darker in the small room. The air became very still and hushed. Florence thought there was going to be a thunderstorm – she had better fetch Ann in. She was still sleeping on her back, so Florence pushed the pram inside the house - just in time, as the rain was falling faster and faster and the drops were the size of pennies. Then came a flash of lightning, followed some time later by a roar of thunder.

Florence had counted the seconds between the lightning and thunder, and felt the centre of the storm was still some distance away. She went inside the house, closing the door firmly behind her. She went through a thick curtain which served as a 'door' from the small hall to the sitting room. She picked up an old *Farmers' Weekly*, well out of date but it would be something to read whilst she put her feet up on the sofa. She read about the best time to harvest, what a poor year it had been for everything and what a disastrous year it had been for potatoes.

Then Frank began to wake.

"There's a bad thunderstorm" she said. "I brought Ann into the house, she's still asleep in the pram."

Frank stood up and came over to the sofa. Florence felt very panicky, but he only wanted to sit beside her, which was a big relief.

"I need to tell you what Jack Harrison is going to do" he said. "He wants to begin at the beginning of September and will finish it by the winter."

"Before you start, would you like a cup of tea? You were snoring like pigs going to market."

"All right, I am a bit dry."

Florence went to make tea in the kitchen, thinking what a change to Frank alcohol made. She took two cups into the sitting room and sat down on the sofa.

"Well, tell me all."

"Firstly, let me tell you that the Harrison quote was the best, though not the cheapest. I feel we both want the same for 98. Jack thinks the two houses should be joined across the top, opening the centre up so we can get down to the old stables, leaving enough room for the carriages to get down. Then we'll have a glass roof put up above the last hundred yards so the carriages can be parked under there in the dry. Jack has suggested we have this new electric lighting put in, he's sure everyone will have it soon. He also thinks we should have two shop fronts, one either side of the arch. What do you think?"

"Goodness me Frank, that's going to cost an awful lot of money, where will we get it from? I like the sound of having electricity and not having to negotiate that narrow entry. It was supposed to be the width of a horse, but it must have been a very narrow horse, that's what I think."

"Well it'll all be better soon, thank heavens."

Florence thought this was the best conversation they had had for months.

"Our parents are here tomorrow, please don't go for a drink tonight" she said.

"You feed, and do whatever you have to do with Ann, and I will go for a walk, I could do with some fresh air now the storm has passed, it even smells fresher in here, doesn't it?"

Florence knew he was eventually going for a drink, but maybe the rest of the family would see how they were now. Ann needed a cuddle, a bit of attention, as she had been in the hall in the pram for over an hour.

"Frank, would you go and fetch Ann please?"

"You go, I need to go to the toilet. Which reminds me, I forgot to tell you that Jack's planning to erect a toilet off the landing, suspended in mid-air!"

Frank still hadn't held Ann, something else which was not right. She was a week old. She would have a word with her father over dinner.

She went to the darkened hallway and picked the baby up. Ann was warm and sleepy and Florence was saddened with Frank's choice.

Frank appeared and said he was going for a walk. Florence knew she would be in bed when she saw him next, and she was.

Florence was up twice in the night with Ann. The next morning she looked over at the jaundiced Frank and really hoped his parents would take him to task about his appearance; they would surely see a change in him.

She dressed and went to feed and dress Ann. When she had done that she carried her down the back stairs, forgetting the big step at the bottom – she had to sit down and touch the edge to put her feet on the floor - and put the baby in the pram, which was still in the hall.

She pushed the pram outside. It looked like a fine, sunny day. First she would fetch the vegetables and meat from the cellar, a part of the house she disliked intensely. Frank had bought this house because it was close to the new great Central station, and it was an old property, full of mice. Just a week before she had been down to the cellar to get some potatoes from a hessian sack and had taken a basket down with her. When she looked at them in the kitchen there was a dead mouse among the potatoes. Now there was a pair of gloves permanently left down there.

Picking up the well-used tray and a lit candle, she opened the door and, singing at the top of her voice (anything to scare the mice), she went down. The steps were steep, made of brick and a crumbling in places. The white metal-meshed meat safe was just at the bottom of the stairs. It would be so much better when they had some electric light down here.

She loaded the tray - why hadn't she brought the basket, she wondered? Then, with a candle lighting the way, she climbed back up.

Just as she reached the door at the top of the stairs, there was a knock at the front door which was almost opposite. "Come on in, Annie" Florence called. She carried the tray through the heavy floor-length curtain which served as a door. Then she heard a commotion and pulled the curtain to one side - to see Annie lying face down on the hall floor. She gasped in horror.

"Annie, are you all right?" What a stupid thing to say, she thought. Of course she wasn't, she had fallen! "Let me help you to your feet, then we'll go and sit at the table and you can recover a bit, do you hurt anywhere? I'll get you a glass of water."

When she came back she looked at Annie. " What happened?"

"I was determined to be on time" said Annie. "I heard you call 'Come in', so I did, but I tripped over the threshold as I came, I'm so sorry."

"Do you feel better?"

"I'm OK now thanks, what do you want me to do?"

"If you're sure you're all right, I'd like you to get the potatoes peeled and parboiled first please." She showed Annie to the kitchen, realising how small it was. "I'll go and set the table - there will be seven of us Annie, do all the veg. Please."

Annie took out from her carrier bag a floral material 'coat' which Annie put on and wrapped around her body and tied it behind her back with thin tapes. Annie said, "Shall I begin with the potatoes, Mrs Ginns?"

"Yes please, Mr Ginns was out until late last night, I'll just go and see if he is up, then check the back bedroom – my mother may be staying a few days, her name is Mrs Cambers. Oh, of course you know that."

Florence went up the front stairs. They were shallow, wide steps with a banister made of shiny mahogany with a swirl at the bottom. She went into the bedroom to find Frank washing his face.

"Morning, did you have a good walk? Annie's here working, when you come down you'll see her. Your parents will be here soon, you know mother may stay on don't you? I am just going to check the back bedroom, see you downstairs."

That was enough. She didn't want to talk to him, really. She went through her aunt's room along a small corridor into the back bedroom. The huge feather mattress lay on the bed, two feather pillows, a sheet, two woolly Witney blankets and an old piece of patchwork lay over it all. As yet there was little else in the room except for the chamber pot.

Florence opened the sash and then went down the back stairs, opened the door at the bottom and cursing her dress as she lowered herself to the floor.

"Mrs Johnson, how are you getting on? Mr Ginns will be down soon. I am going to lay the table, is the joint in? This oven is very old, to be honest, we've never cooked in it before. Please remember when the time comes, to see the fat is sizzling hot. I made the batter yesterday, have you seen it?"

"Oh Mrs Ginns, I saw the basin and was going to throw it away, as you said it is a small kitchen I was making room, I'm sorry."

"All you need to do is whisk it again before pouring into the hot fat, as I said."

"Yes, I will try."

Frank made his appearance, telling Annie she had obviously accepted the job, for which he was grateful as she would definitely be a help to Mrs Ginns. "Tomorrow morning you will meet Charlie Hancock" he said. "He arrives early to clean the shoes and lay and light the fires. He used to be a groom. When he is concentrating on some cleaning he makes a noise through his teeth, maybe what he used to do when he was grooming horses. He seems a good chap, keeps himself to himself. He has taken over the downstairs of number 100. We are having Mr Harrison from next to the church to do the front, and an upstairs toilet - when he's finished a horse and carriage will be able to go down to the stables. You know him, surely? When the family arrive my father is bringing them over in one of his carriages. I arranged with J... I mean Mr Harrison, to leave it there whilst they have dinner."

Frank went to open the door, expecting to see five excited faces, but they were all looking into the pram at their week-old granddaughter and niece. Francis had hacked over and was holding the reins of his favourite horse, Drambuie.

"Father, I have arranged with Mr Harrison for you to park the carriage in his yard. He is a good man, he will be doing the alterations very soon."

"Oh my word, she looks beautiful, and what a lot of hair! When should she wake up?"

"Mother, don't be so impatient. She should wake soon. Come in and I'll ask Annie, our new housekeeper, to get us some. I haven't laid the table yet as there's not a lot of room, so as soon as she wakes, you can hold her."

Walking into the house, the ladies took their hats off and put them on a table in the hall, to be joined by the men's. Florence went to see how Annie was, putting the kettle on as she did so. All was fine, Annie was fine, and hopefully the pudding was fine, too.

Florence smiled to herself and thought she would just let them enjoy Ann alone for a while. Frank had gone to the Harrisons' with the carriage and Francis was back from the stables. Florence made tea for all, then carried it in on the tray, by which time all were back. Ann needed feeding and by the smell of her, changing too.

Ann was passed around the family, with many an 'ooh,' and 'Isn't she lovely! She will break some man's heart one day."

"She'll break mine if I don't change and feed her" said Florence. "Are the two grandmothers coming up with me? I shall need a bit of help with this dress before feeding her. We can use the front stairs, they're easier."

"How are you, Florence? You look quite tired. Do you get much help?"

"I'm glad Mrs. Johnson has begun today, I have felt very lonely. Are you able to stay, mother?"

"I am until Wednesday afternoon."

"I too feel you don't look very well, but it's only been a week" said Mrs Ginns Senior. Little do you know, thought Florence.

"I've been busy, we need to talk about several things over

dinner, including Ann's cot, something has to be done, you'll see in a minute."

When the two grandmas saw the 'crib' they were aghast. "For goodness sake, the poor child deserves a proper cot, why don't you have one? If you feel too busy, or tired. Why didn't Frank buy or make one?"

"I agree with your mother" said Florence. She didn't say much, but what she said was well thought out. "Well, I wasn't going to tell you, but Frank has never picked Ann up, or held her, it makes me so sad, what can I do? Please help me."

"Oh Florence, my dear, we both felt things weren't right, didn't we?"

"Indeed we did, we thought maybe it was Frank's health. He's looking very yellow, has he been to the doctor? I know it's not cheap, but there's something that needs looking at, I think."

"So do I, I keep saying to go to the doctor's but it's like talking to a brick wall. What do I do? I am so lonely, all my friends are still in Belgrave. I did bump into Penny in Loseby Lane on Wednesday. I'd like to ask her to be one of Ann's godmothers. I'm asking my friend Agnes too, but the vicar is coming to see us to finalise arrangements. On Tuesday you will still be here, won't you mother?"

"Yes, I will on Tuesday, perhaps we can go shopping in Leicester tomorrow. That would be a good idea, is there anything you want?"

"I'd like to have a look in the Beehive on Cank Street. I need some more curtains, and some blue Silko and a new pack of sewing machine needles. I have a lot of sewing to do when I get home."

"Now I've changed Ann, will you help me with my dress please? After I've fed her I'll be down and we can eat, if the men are back. Mother, would you check with Annie that all is well with the cooking? Everything for the table is around the kitchen, which isn't very big, as you'll see. First, just have a look at your room, it's through this door two or three paces and that's it. You can go down the back stairs, but someone will have to help you down after the door at the bottom – you'll be back in the sitting room."

"I'll go and sort downstairs out, then, if the men are back, maybe Frank can show the others what we are planning to do."

Florence found it easier to manage her dress by pulling first one side then the other to feed Ann. She decided to go back down the front stairs, as it was far more elegant. When she arrived downstairs she discovered that the men had just arrived, and Frank was proudly showing them around. The two women had almost set the table, a gate-legged oval oak table which didn't leave much room around it. Chairs were brought from what was going to become the downstairs office. Now all was ready. Florence squeezed through to the kitchen, to see how Annie was.

"Annie, have you managed? It hasn't been a very good start for you, has it? I'm sorry I haven't been around to help you much."

"I do understand, Mrs Ginns, the only thing I couldn't find was the pepper and enough plates, do you have more?"

"There are some, but where they are I don't know. I'll have a look. There are some boxes still unpacked in the room that's going to our office. Leave your apron on, they know you're at work."

A few minutes later Annie came back hugging an armful of plates. "Mrs Ginns, you have quite a few more left in there still, I will just wash these, when the water has boiled" she said.

The men returned, and Ann was put in her pram outside. Everyone found a chair, the men sat down and the three ladies brought the food out. It was a lovely piece of beef, well worth the walk. Florence thought she would use Raggs again.

"It is so lovely to see everyone, isn't it Frank? We have a lot to tell you - ask you. Firstly, Father, please could Jack Johnson have some wood from you to make a much-needed cot for Ann?" She looked over at the two grandmas. "And any others that may follow."

"Of course he can have some wood, let your mother bring a note with her when she comes home. Is Jack Annie's husband?"

"Yes he is, though we have yet to meet him."

"I hope you liked what we're planning to do with number 98 at the beginning of next month. I will be so pleased to be able to get down to the stables from Highcross Street. Won't be long now, Jack Harrison says. I miss driving my carriages."

"The other thing we need to discuss is Ann's christening. I went to All Saints just after she was born, the vicar was away but he's calling round on Tuesday – you'll still be here, mother, so you can help, it's really which date and who to invite really. I spoke to the churchwarden, a Mr Gutteridge, when I went. He seems a really good man, lives on St Nicholas Street, said he'd call in now and again, so perhaps you may meet him, Mother."

Florence didn't need to mention William but it made her feel a bit happier.

"I hope we can have it before the builders get going, I think we will have 'the party here for just a few friends and family. Frank, I have chosen the two godmothers, who would you like to be Ann's godfather?"

"Francis?"

"Shall we try to arrange it about three o'clock on the first free Sunday in September? I think three is a good time for you to get over. There are relations in Hathern we should ask too. What about you, Frank?"

"I don't know, ask my parents while they're here."

"There won't be many, most of our relations live too far away to ride down" said Mrs Ginns.

"Will you let me have their addresses? Then when we have seen Rev. Swingler on Tuesday we can invite them."

"I will, but, as I said, there won't be many."

The beef was maybe a little overcooked, and the Yorkshire – what had she done with it? She hadn't a clue – she had done the batter right, so why did it have the consistency of shoe leather?

"I'm very sorry about the meal, I promise I'll cook next time" she said.

Her mother replied quickly, "It was your first attempt in a new house, with a new oven and a new person to help you cook. I think we all agree you were being very ambitious, don't we?"

Frank's father spoke for the first time for a while. "We all feel you've done really well so far, and we are all behind you both, all the way, aren't we?"

Florence excused herself and went to the kitchen.

"Mrs Johnson, thank you for your help, it was difficult for us all today" she said. "If you would ask Jack to call round with a note of what wood he needs, Mother will take it with her when she leaves on Wednesday afternoon. She's catching the bus from St Margaret's at four o'clock."

As Florence was speaking Mrs Johnson was peeling the apron off and hanging it on a hook which was conveniently behind the back door, which led to the toilet and the new tin bath. Florence put the kettle on to make everyone a drink, and asked Mrs Johnson if she would treat today as a 'special'.

"And then will you begin proper work tomorrow? Between nine and twelve every weekday. That's what we agreed, isn't it? Oh, one more thing. There is a Charlie Hancock who you'll meet tomorrow. He lets himself in early in the morning and lights the fires. He has based himself downstairs in number 100. I will see you tomorrow at nine o'clock. I'll get Jack to sort out how much wood he will need, he is looking forward to making it, you'll meet him soon, though."

There was steam coming from the kettle. Florence made yet more tea and carried it to the table. The plates had been piled up to go to the pig swill in the kitchen.

"I think it's time we should be thinking of starting back to Belgrave" said Mrs Ginns.

"Don't forget my bag from the carriage, Frank" said Mrs Cambers.

Once the tea had been drunk, Francis went to fetch his horse from the stables, kissed goodbye to Florence and Mrs Cambers and had a look at Ann, soon to be his godchild, then he was seen walking Drambuie through the entry and mounting him on Highcross Street. Mr Ginns went to the Harrisons' for the carriage, which was really a brougham, and stopped directly outside 98.

"I'm sure there'll be some changes when we come to the christening" said Mr Cambers.

CHAPTER THREE

Frank took Flo's mother's heavy Gladstone bag up to her room and put it firmly on the bed, denting the feather mattress. Mrs Cambers and Florence had cleared the table and the kitchen and had just sat in the sitting room.

"Well that all went well, didn't it?" said Mrs Cambers.

"The dinner wasn't as good as I'd hoped, I am sorry, next time I'll try to cook myself."

Frank appeared. "Oh hello, I see peace reigns, that's good."

"Would you just go and see if Ann's still asleep please?"

"She'll be all right, she's not crying."

Florence shot a look at her mother and then went outside herself.

"What are you doing this evening dear?"

"Well I knew your mother was here, so I am meeting a few of my Glooston shooting friends, at the Hat and Beaver for a change."

"That's a long way from Glooston. How many will there be, do you think?"

"Well, I think Dick Harvey and Ray McDowie will be there and probably Steve, you know, Steve Allen, if his wife will let him off the leash."

"Oh, you haven't seen them since the last shoot, have you? What about Paul? What's become of him?"

"He's bought a pub in Earl Shilton, apparently it's very busy a lot of the time so he seems to have moved on. Earl Shilton is the wrong side of Leicester."

"We're seeing the vicar at 11.30 tomorrow - if you can be here, good, then we are going shopping in town."

"I have to go to St. Martin's, to the bank to sort out some money for Jack Harrison before he starts. I'll get there as soon as I can."

"We'll be fine. We'll probably go to bed before we have to put the lights on. Ann will need feeding and bathing before she goes to bed."

"Can I help you dear?" said Kate. "I am her grandma, after all."

Florence knew she had to go and check that Annie would still be able to help on Sunday, then she had to go to the market, to Lineker's stall for the green veg, as there was a whole sack of potatoes in the cellar; she remembered they had been put there last week, when they'd moved in, and thought what a strange thing to bring with them. She pushed the pram up to the top of Highcross Street, glancing down at the red granite cross in the road which marked where the original centre of Leicester was until the recently constructed Clock Tower was finished. Florence quite wanted to see it. Apparently there were four statues, one on each corner, of famous Leicester personalities.

When she had seen the Clock Tower she went into the market. She had never noticed the cobbles until now, pushing a pram. They made her feel a bit fatigued. Leicester Market was very old, she remembered, begun around 1300 if not before. There were at least a hundred stalls and all the stallholders were shouting, trying to attract customers, but Florence blanked them out. She only needed veg from Lineker's, then home. She bought leeks, parsnips and carrots and decided to go back past the fish market; she loved looking at the fish, sardines, plaice and haddock, all staring with unseeing eyes.

At last the cobbles ended and flat pavements began. She had decided to walk back down Loseby Lane when she bumped into Penny Webb, a very old friend.

"Oh, Penny, lovely to see you, in fact better than you can imagine" she said.

"Yes, and your new baby, is it a girl or a boy? Can I see?"

"A girl, she's almost a week old. Penny, I really need to talk. Can we meet very soon? At this moment I'm very tired and Ann needs feeding, so I have to hurry, shall we meet for lunch?"

"I'll book a table at the Turkey Café in Granby Street. I like it there, do you? But I'll let you go, you do look tired. See you soon." They waved and went off in different directions.

The pram was harder to push now, but at least it was downhill. Florence arrived home and really needed a drink, and Ann needed one too, so she sat on the sofa and fed her, then took her upstairs to change her and put her in the drawer to sleep. Florence felt tired too, so she went to the bedroom and lay down fully dressed in her favourite black taffeta dress which she'd bought when Queen Victoria had died.

The next thing she realised was that Frank was standing beside the bed, looking very aroused. He pushed her across so he could lie beside her.

"Frank, you've been patient, but it has been less than a week and we can do other things. No, stop it, you're hurting me!"

"I don't care, I'm having you now."

"Frank, no, Frank please!" She heard her dress rip. "Please don't, it's so soon, wait Frank!"

But Frank took no notice. There were more sounds of tearing and gasps and screams from Florence as Frank had his way with her, satisfying his needs. Florence cried silently to herself.

Frank lay sleeping for a while, and Florence lay very still and very quiet when her tears had ended. All she wanted was to be left alone and to wash herself and get him out of her. She wondered what on earth she had married, and what she should do now.

Frank dressed quickly and disappeared downstairs, obviously going for another drink somewhere. When she heard the front door close she sat up to see that her dress had been ripped to pieces, and her tears welled up again. But she had things to do. She emptied the jug of cold water which she'd put there two days before - she would get the new housekeeper to do it soon. She looked for something with which to wipe him away. The only thing she could see was an antimacassar on the back of the fireside chair. With that she washed herself as much as she could. Then she went to the kitchen and put the kettle on to boil. Once it had boiled she washed herself thoroughly with hot water and carbolic soap, dried herself well and felt much better. Tomorrow would be better.

She was so glad when the christening guests had all gone. Only her mother remained, but she would be more of a help than a hindrance, and Mrs Johnson would be back tomorrow. Then Reverend Swingler and maybe Mr Gutteridge too would be here on Tuesday. She felt a faint tremor of excitement.

Later, when Florence and her mother were alone, she had the chance at last to discuss her worries.

"Mother, you how do you and Father think Frank looks? I am so afraid about him, but he won't go to see Dr Angus. He is so yellow and sleeps a lot, and his eyes are getting more and more bloodshot. Mother, what's wrong with him? What should I do?"

"Florence, my dear Florence, your husband is an alcoholic. He may not live for long, he must be drinking so much."

"But there is more, Mother, wait there a minute, I'll show you." She stood up and went upstairs, gathered up the torn fragments of her dress and laid them before her mother.

"And this is what he did the other day" she said.

"But this was a fine dress. What on earth happened?"

Florence took a very deep breath, knowing the enormity of what she was about to say.

"Frank did it to me and the dress a few days ago, he had had a drink and he came over to me and said he had been patient for long enough. I said it was too early, so he just… he raped me. Oh Mother, what can I do?"

"Florence, your father and I just thought it was Frank's health, but this is far worse. Can I tell your father?"

"What will he do about it? If you must, but no one else, I feel ashamed and dirty even though I have had a good wash. He just keeps trying whenever he's had a drink, what shall I do?"

"First thing you do is go to see Dr Angus, you can be honest with him. Make an appointment with him as soon as you can. Either Mrs Johnson or I will look after Ann."

"Well I must get help, mustn't I? I'll go over tomorrow morning."

"That's good, I'm glad I stayed for longer, your pa and I thought it was his health that was the problem, but not this. How old is he 27, 28 ? He's always liked a drink, I remember him as a young boy in The Dolphin. He liked a tipple then."

"I know Mother, but he's changed. Maybe I shouldn't have told you. Please don't tell anyone but Father. And tell him to tell no one, not even Jeff Manning, I know he's known him for a long time but no…"

Flo's ever-practical mother then said, "Get a big bag, I'll take it all upstairs and if you give me an old tin and some scissors I will sit on that wonderful thick feather mattress and cut all the Whitby jet beads off and I am sure Mrs Johnson will throw the rest away somewhere. So sad Florence, I know you loved it, but I'm sure you will be glad to see it gone. I will."

"Mr Swingler has left, can we have a look in Morley's to see what dresses they have in there?"

"I think it would be a good idea, to be honest it didn't fit you as well now Ann's arrived."

Florence put the fraying pieces into an old paper bag, with scissors and an old custard tin. It was a little rusty but fine for jet beads, thought Florence.

"Ma, I think I told you but remember Charlie Hancock will be here early tomorrow morning? He has a key. He is really here to get the fires lit and clean the shoes and brasses. Now I need to go to bed Mother. It will be easier if you use the back stairs. I'll help you up the first step, Frank's put your bag on your bed. I'm sorry, there isn't much in there yet, I have put a jug of water in there though and a gazunda if you need it." The gazunda was of course for use in the night, so called because it 'gazunda' the bed.

"Can I just have a glass of water?"

"I'll get it now." With that, Florence helped her mother up the huge first step of the back stairs, handed her her water, wished her goodnight and promised she would go to the doctor's in the morning. The lights were being lit in Highcross Street. She lay and wondered what her mother was thinking.

Florence awoke early to the sound of Charlie clearing out the fire in the sitting room, the only fire they were lighting at the moment. Frank was still snoring beside her, loudly, she thought, for his age. She decided to wear an ordinary work dress today and an apron; she knew she would have to show Annie around a bit.

She went into Ann's room; it was the first time she had woken before her daughter. She fed, changed and dressed her in a pretty pink dress, then went to the back stairs and softly knocked on her mother's door.

"Come in, Flo."

"Morning Mother, how did you sleep? Well, I hope, on that mattress. Here you go, Grandma Kate, I'll go down and make us some tea. Still two cubes for you?"

"Only one now, Flo."

"Right, enjoy your eight-day-old granddaughter while I make the tea. Would you like a biscuit? We have pink wafers, you used to like them."

"Lovely, thank you, now leave me with Ann."

Florence went down the back stairs and negotiated the bottom step, without looking at herself in the mahogany oval mirror Frank had recently put up over the fireplace in the sitting room, the fireplace which Charlie had recently cleaned and woken Florence whilst doing it. The kettle would soon boil, so while waiting Florence prepared the tray. Then, putting the tray on the third step up the stairs, she gathered her dress up and went up with the tray to have tea with her mother on the mattress. Annie would be here soon and her mother would need breakfast. Boiled eggs came to mind – but where were the egg cups?

"Annie will be here very soon, once she is here I will go over to the doctor's and leave Ann with you whilst I go. Is that all right? I'll take Ann down, just call at the bottom and I'll take the tray from you."

"I'll be down in a minute."

Again Florence went down, leaving the tray for her mother to bring down. Then she went to have a look for some egg cups in the unpacked wooden crates in the 'office'. After about ten minutes she heard her mother calling and went to relieve her of the tray. Mrs Johnson could have a look for them when she arrived. Mother would have toast and jam, she knew where the pot was.

"I was going to give you a boiled egg but I can't find the egg cups so it'll have to be quince jelly and toast, sorry."

Florence put Ann in the hall. It looked a bit overcast outside, so she left her in the pram in the hall. She was about to go and rouse Frank when he appeared on the stairs, looking unkempt and exhausted, even after a night's sleep. His pallor and bloodshot eyes made her glad she was going to see Dr Angus later.

"Morning dear, you slept well. Remember Annie Johnson begins here this morning and remember too, Mother is here. I have to go out this morning. I will leave Ann with Mother. What are you doing?"

"Flo, I've only just woken up, let me have a wash and some breakfast then I'll tell you what I'm doing."

"All right" said Florence, and left him to it. They both went through to the kitchen, which seemed to be getting smaller each time she saw it.

"I'm making a pot of tea, will you come and have breakfast with us?"

"Sounds a good idea."

There came the sound of knocking, then a key being turned from outside. Annie Johnson let herself in, followed by a tall, thin young man.

"Mrs Ginns, Mr Ginns, this is my husband Jack, he's come with measurements of the wood for the cot."

"Please Jack, go through, my mother is there."

"Annie, hopefully things will be more peaceful for you now! We are about to have breakfast, then I will show you around. While we eat please would you look in the 'office' and see if you can find some egg cups. You were good yesterday. If you do, please leave them in there until we have more space. Now, we must speak to Jack."

"At last we meet. Thank you very much for agreeing to let Annie help when our daughter was born last week and for offering to make the much-needed cot" said Frank, who was looking better since he'd washed and put a collar and tie on.

"Mother, I have had a thought, do you think it may be easier if Jack came over to Belgrave and made it there?"

"It would be quicker and easier for me" said Jack.

"We have what equipment and wood he will need, that's a good idea. When could you come?"

"I could come over and make it next Saturday, then if we can finish it back here, if you give me your address I will come by bus next Saturday – I work at Byford's during the week otherwise."

Mrs Cambers took a card from her handbag and handed it to Mr Johnson. "See you on Saturday then."

Jack went back to the kitchen, where Annie, once again wearing her overall, almost bumped into him.

"I must hurry, I'll talk tonight, be good." With a rush he was gone.

They finished their breakfast, slightly interrupted by Annie going in to the office to look for egg cups. Frank said, "I am seeing Perry and Newton this morning, how long will you be?"

"Not too long I don't think, why?"

"Well, we need to decide on the front of number 98. You usually have good ideas, expensive but good, will you find us when you get back?"

"Yes, of course I will." She was feeling glad to be involved. Florence put on her hat, bade farewell to them both, looked at Ann, who was still sleeping, and went out through the narrow entrance to Highcross Street, walking uphill for about 60 yards. She crossed over to a Regency house, complete with a fanlight above the front door. Ringing the doorbell, she let herself into a hallway. The floor was slate slabs, the ceiling was high. At the far end was a staircase with a window showing trees wafting in the breeze, maybe a garden. Florence wished number 98 had a garden. The wall on the left faced the door to the surgery. There was a mother and baby waiting, but luckily no one else. Florence wondered how much this was going to cost, but she needed someone outside the family to help.

Eventually Dr Angus called her in. "How can I help?"

"Good morning Doctor Angus. My husband and I have just moved into number 98 three weeks ago, and since then I have had a baby. I will bring her for you to check, but really it's about my husband, two things really. First of all he looks very yellow to me. My mother, who is staying with us at the moment, says it is his liver. His eyes are bloodshot and he sleeps a lot. My mother says he drinks too much. So I am very worried about that; he won't come to see you, just says he is fine.

"The other thing is" – she felt herself become hot and flushed – when he has had too much liquor he rapes me, well, he has once, but he won't leave me alone. Please, please help me."

"How old is he?"

"He's only a couple of months older than me, 28."

"Well unless he makes an appointment I can do very little, Mrs Ginns, but you must encourage him to come and see me as soon as you can. Maybe I could call in to see the baby."

"If you could call around, Doctor, I am very worried, about him and myself too."

Florence retraced her steps and found Frank in discussion with a short man with dressed in work clothes.

"Mr Newton, this is my wife. She is going to have some input with the design."

"Mr Newton, how do you do? I must just go to see if my mother is all right, then I will be straight back, excuse me."

Florence went inside. Ann was being changed by her grandmother. Mrs Johnson was looking on as if she had wanted to do it.

"Mrs Ginns, you were quick, Ann has only just woken. I couldn't find your egg cups, but they're probably at the bottom of one of those crates."

"Grandma Kate, I can see you've been a good grandma, thank you for looking after her. No rain, so she can go out Annie, please. Now I need to join the men outside, excuse me Mother, I won't be long."

"Making number 98 similar to Churchgate I think would be an excellent idea," she told Mr Newton. "But I would need there to be some differences, so they won't look too similar. I would like black and white tiles, discreet, in the entrance. What do you think, dear? The kitchen needs enlarging. Goodness, there is so much to do. I think we need to complete the front first. Most of the rest must wait. First the yard to the stables must be covered, Mr Harrison will be here in ten days remember.

"Shall we go to Morley's, mother? Ann can stay with Annie. Is that all right Annie? mother just needs to go to the Beehive, shouldn't be long."

They prepared to go, putting on their hats. They felt free.

"Let's go and get what you need from the Beehive, then a look in Morley's, shall we?"

The Beehive was one of Florence's favourite shops. It had lots of stock displayed on shelves which went from the floor to ceiling with lots of material of all patterns and thicknesses; woollen, cotton, denim, gingham and velvet. However, the best feature was the way you paid. The money and invoice were put in a brass cylinder which the sales person 'pinged' up a wire to the cashiers up above.

They found the needles and everything else and paid for it, then they went beside the market to Morley's to look for a new dress to replace the black taffeta. Of course Frank would pay. When they arrived at Morley's Florence noted how bright and new it was compared to the Beehive. The dresses were upstairs, a thin shop assistant told them, men's clothing only downstairs. Typical, thought Florence as they trailed up the marble staircase – always easier for men.

The department had many dresses, some with the latest fashion, a bustle' which Florence quite fancied as it would hide her 'derrière'. Eventually she found a dress in pink, scattered with sprigs of darker pink roses and a few dark green leaves. Both of them thought it a good choice, ideal for the mother of the baby. All they now needed was a hat, bag and shoes, then they could go back to number 98.

"I have a dark pink shawl in Belgrave, I'll bring it over when I come. Now what about a hat? You love hats don't you? They must have them on this floor."

It didn't take long for Florence to find which hat; she chose one in dark pink, with a small bunch of roses on the front. If you waited a week they would put a ribbon on it, in the colour of your choice – Florence chose a cream satin one, then changed her mind to a dark pink satin one. After paying, all on account of course, they went back for a chat about the christening: Rev Swingler would be there tomorrow.

Frank was there, mulling over their expenses, and Florence thought it better not to mention her new dress and hat until they arrived. Since the black taffeta incident she had spoken to him when he was sober and was more prepared when he insisted, quite frequently. He was sick of him pawing her at every opportunity, but she kept her thoughts to herself.

Wednesday arrived cool and sunny. Flo's mother was late appearing, and Florence supposed she had been packing. Then she showed up at the bottom of the back stairs with her filled bag and her gazunda, which she took to empty in the toilet.

There was a knock at the front door and Frank appeared looking very clean and tidy. Then the Vicar and Mr Gutteridge arrived. Annie made tea for them all after introductions had been made; Florence was a little flustered when Frank introduced William to her mother. Why, she wondered. Then she realised; he seemed such a good man, unlike Frank, who was out for himself first, second and last. William seemed kind as far has she could tell. He'd held Ann, whereas Frank hadn't held her at all.

They all sat down around the table. Rev. Swingler began, "First things first I was thinking we could hold it on Sunday August the 30th, when Ann will be two weeks old, at three o'clock."

"That's what we were thinking. We know who we're having as godparents so we can ask them formally now. Mother is going back to Belgrave today, so she can tell friends there, but there won't be many Ginns as most of the family live in Leeds. mother and I will write the invitations before she goes."

"You have a great deal to do, so we will leave you. Thank you for the tea. I'll see you on the 30th if not before." He was looking straight at Florence.

"We need to formally invite Penny Webb, Agnes Hanson and

brother Francis, then those Cambers who live in Weston-under-Dunsmore" replied Florence. "Shall we get them written now? Then Ann and I will walk with you to St Margaret's bus station. I really will miss you. Please will you and Father come over the day before and help move things out of the way?"

"I'll wash and starch my christening dress, it's a family tradition which I would hate to end. I'll just sort Ann out and then we can write the letters and the invitations and get them posted."

"I'll be getting on with the invitations, and by the way the Cambers' relations live in Hathern, not Weston under Dunsmore. They have even planted two red rose bushes by the wall in the churchyard, so look if you ever go over. I have their addresses with me in my bag ready to take back to Belgrave. I'll get on with them. I don't think there will be many of the Ginns being up in Leeds. Do you want it to be at 98 or at the new Victory public house?"

"We'll have to move the packing cases over to number 100, then we'll have enough room. You and Father are coming over on the Saturday still, aren't you? Please can you make the cake, Ma? Annie is proving to be a godsend, but her cookery skills need a lot of honing I am afraid. What else? Champagne, only two or three bottles will be enough, but I know Frank will organise the liquor!"

"I'm so sorry Florence to be leaving you with him. He is a very ill man but he won't do anything about it. I know you've tried. He is heading for a fall, but how you are going to cope with the black taffeta business, I don't know. You've spoken to the doctor about it. It is all basically his drinking."

"I've told you Ma, I just give in to him now, and don't lie on the bed wearing my favourite dress! But he likes it."

The letters were written and envelopes stamped ready for posting at St Margaret's. Then a letter arrived for Florence. It was from Penny, saying she'd booked a table for three at the Turkey Café. Florence thought how much Ann would love having her two godmothers so close to each other and two sets of grandparents in Belgrave too.

"Mother, Jack Johnson will be coming over to make Ann's cradle, perhaps we will pay him as a christening present. You ask Mr Ginns if he could bring it with him when they come to the christening please?"

"Come on Flo, I don't want to miss the bus. I'll get my shoes on, did I bring my parasol?"

"Yes Mother, I put it all away before the Reverend came. You'd left everything in the hall. I just have to change Ann, then we can look, we'll go down High Street. If we go in plenty of time we can have a cup of tea."

She called carelessly ""Frank, we are off now", and Florence and her mother pushed Ann into Highcross Street. Florence realised that Frank hadn't appeared to bid her mother farewell, but she knew there was no love lost between them so she hadn't called him again.

"Can I have a look in Griffins', dear?" asked her mother. "I'd like a new frying pan."

They went to the Bell Hotel for afternoon tea, then went down Belgrave Road, turning left to St Margaret's bus station. It was a hive of activity there with horses being changed. Their sweaty bodies looked wet and steam rose from them. There was a man wearing a green apron, a large shovel and wheelbarrow clearing up any manure. Queues of people waited for buses or alighted from them, and all in all it was chaos. Very noisy too, with horses impatient to be moving, hooves clomping, but standing still. Florence saw the horses' steaming breath and felt sad for them, but she was soon shaken from her thoughts by her mother pointing to a stand where a small queue was slowly forming.

"There's Mrs Wallis and Miss Gaulton" she said. "They live in Belgrave, do you remember them? it must be the place."

Florence's heart missed a beat as she realised her ally, her mother, her confidante, would soon have left. Her life would be just Frank, Ann and Annie Johnson.

Her mother's bus came in on time, and Florence and her mother kissed each other and looked into each other's eyes. Not a thing was said, but their eyes told it all.

Florence remembered they hadn't posted the letters, so she found a post box, walked slowly back and turned left up Highcross Street, seeing the comforting shape of All Saints. Should she go in? She decided she would, and left the pram outside. She was grateful to find no one there. She needed quiet to clear her mind and ask God to do the right thing for Frank. She knew he must see Dr Angus quickly.

She bent her head, then went out as she heard a baby's faint cry. "Shush shush Ann, we'll be home in five minutes, shush" she murmured.

As she put her hand on the brass door handle she drew in a deep breath and just hoped he hadn't been over to the Joiners, but no, he had met Dick Harvey at the Leicester Inn opposite the new Clock Tower; they'd met to discuss the dates for the next shooting season. An automobile had gone around the Clock Tower, then driven up High Street, scaring all the horses. "They say they'll take over from carriages soon, but I can't believe that" said Frank. "Smelly noisy things they are. Soon we will be able to get some horses in the stables and a couple of Father's carriages, then we can begin to start advertising and really get going. I'll be glad when money is coming in rather than going out. It's all waiting on Jack Harrison now."

Florence put the kettle on to boil some water. Ann needed a bath, so Florence used an old white enamel bowl and a flannel and Pears' soap. Mrs Johnson had just bought a bar and told Mrs Ginns that it would be good for Ann, as it was so pure it was transparent.

There would be little to do for the next few days. Annie could do the shopping on the Friday. But then, unexpectedly, a very dapper William appeared on Tuesday morning with a cornflower in his buttonhole. He said he was on his way to Dun's Lane but had just called in. Florence said how pleased to see him she was. She asked him if he was working the following Sunday.

"I am, but only in the morning" he said.

"We are wondering if you would like to come to the party here afterwards. Please say you will."

"I would love to. I only work at All Saints in the morning so it would be very enjoyable. Thank you for thinking of me, what present can I bring for Ann?"

"William, there is no need for you to buy her anything, we would like you to come as you have been involved with the christening from the beginning."

"Goodness, the time! I would love to stay longer but they will be wondering where I am at Duns. I must go, remember me to Frank." With that, he and his cornflower button hole were gone.

Florence thought, not for the first time, that coming to 98 must be a slight deviation to get to Duns Lane, so he must have wanted to see her.

Annie was ironing in the sitting room; there was more space there than in the kitchen.

"Oh Mrs Ginns, could I have a word with you, please?" she asked.

"Of course you can, what's wrong?" replied Florence.

"Nothing, it's just to tell you we're having a baby next summer."

"Annie, I'm so happy for you, and Jack too of course. I suppose the making of Ann's cradle put Jack in the mood! I'm looking forward to seeing it on Sunday. You will have the back bedroom ready for my parents on Friday night and I'll give you a shopping list for you to fetch on Friday. How is Jack? Haven't seen him since we asked him to go over and use my father's tools to make the cradle. She is ready to sleep in something bigger than that drawer."

"Jack says it's good and strong, he says it will meet the needs of any more children you may have in the future."

"I'm looking forward to seeing it."

Frank talked to Jack Harrison. "Remember we are having Ann's christening party next Sunday, will you ask the men to be sure they clear up well on Saturday when they finish for the weekend? And now Mr Cambers can park his carriage in the yard rather than at Jack Harrison's things are slowly improving."

"I'll remember to tell them."

Frank felt a little shaky as he went into the house. He must remember to buy the champagne today, as Flo's parents were arriving tomorrow evening, and he wanted everything to be ready. He knew Charlie had almost finished clearing the boxes from the office and putting them into number 100. He realised Annie was shopping tomorrow; no wonder he felt shaky. He had noticed he wasn't as steady as he used to be. Would it affect his shooting, he wondered? Dick and Steve he knew were coming on Sunday. It would soon be the shooting season.

Frank went into the house and found himself ensconced with Florence and Charlie, discussing how many small tables to put out for the christening.

"I'm just going over to Ben Parker's for the glasses for the party, won't be long" he said. Florence thought he'd better remember the champagne as well as the glasses but decided against reminding him.

As expected Frank was gone for a while, but surprisingly he brought the glasses back with him. Florence found the modern saucer-shaped glasses rather than the old-style flutes which she was used to quite ugly and cumbersome, but life moves on.

"Right, I'm going over for the champagne" said Frank. "I asked Ben to get me six bottles."

"Oh Frank that's too much, far too much, we'll have tea with the cake mother's baking. You're mad! Who has paid for them?"

"I had them from him sale or return, the Glooston men like a drink though Flo."

"Well they might, but not on Ann's champagne, we aren't

made of money and we have a lot to pay for very soon, remember."

"I know" came the reply. "I'll put the champagne in the cellar when I bring it from Ben's, that will cool it down until Sunday."

"Remember, Mother and Father are here tomorrow night, they arrive at St Margaret's at a quarter to four, please be around when they arrive."

"I will be at the bank but when they close I will be home soon after, about the same time as they arrive I expect."

"I might take Ann to meet them."

Frank went over to Ben's later and Florence checked her parents' bedroom and saw that there was enough food for them. She knew Annie had everything organised, but once Ann was washed and fed she felt lonely. She knew that once Frank was home she wouldn't be able to feel that way, quite the opposite.

And so it was. Frank was the same as usual, having been drinking, and once again threw himself upon Flo's scantily-clad body. Florence was used to it now. She just let him let him carry on, while she thought of the party.

The next thing Florence knew was Ann crying for food. Frank still snored beside her. Ann was changed and fed, and Florence was glad to think that there would be only two more nights before Ann could have a proper cot. She wondered how they would pay Jack Johnson. She hoped her parents would give the cot to them as a present; she'd know soon enough.

Florence was next awoken by the sound of the Kirby and West milk cart stopping below their bedroom window. She must leave a note for extra milk for Sunday, she thought. The noise awoke Frank too, so they both washed and dressed at the same time, saying little to each other.

"What are you doing at the bank today?"

"I'm just going over our expenses and how much we must borrow, and over how long we will have to repay it. I am seeing a Mr Hooper. Are you going to St. Margaret's?"

"I think I will, Ann's grown a bit in the two weeks since they last saw her, I suppose I want to show her off."

"Who will be here?"

"Nobody. Last one to leave must lock up, it'll be me I expect, don't forget to take your key too. I'm just going to check that Annie has her shopping list, then I can concentrate on Ann. What are you doing this morning? You're looking very yellow. You slept well last night though."

"I feel a bit tired and shaky sometimes, but don't tell me to go to the doctor's Florence, it will go away, I'm sure. Your parents are here in a few hours, aren't they?"

"They will. Why haven't you spoken to me about how you feel before? I really think you should see the doctor. Please Frank, for me if not for yourself, go to the doctor's."

"I'll leave it until I get one of Father's carriages here, then I'll see. That's what I'm doing this morning. I'll make sure the builders leave the entrance clear so Father can use the old stables and leave his carriage down there instead of at Jack Harrison's."

Florence went into the kitchen. She had to hunt around for Annie's shopping list and was just looking through it when a poorly-looking Annie arrived.

"Morning Annie, whatever's the matter?"

"Morning sickness Mrs Ginns, I'm so sorry." At that she dashed to the sink.

"Are you sure you're well enough to work?"

"I am sure, it's probably finished now."

"I think you'll have a boy, we'll see!"

"I don't mind, I just wish it would stop."

"The shopping list is fine, I'm going to meet my parents this afternoon, Mr Ginns is out too. Will you put the shopping in the meat safe in the cellar? Mother and I will do it all on Sunday morning?"

Florence heard Frank go out, and decided to put Ann outside. Though it was still cloudy, it was warm. Ann had recently discovered her thumb and she lay there sucking it, making an appealing quiet gurgling sound as she sucked. Florence listened for a moment, then took herself upstairs. She wanted to see her new dress and maybe try it on again.

Then she heard the front door open and close. She called downstairs, knowing that whoever it was wouldn't be able to hear her. There was silence, a heavy silence, and then she heard him walking up the stairs. She knew it was Frank and her heart missed a beat. She knew what he wanted, but this time she had her new dress on, which he hadn't seen before.

"Right, you can get that off" he said. "Don't suppose you want it to go the same way as that black one, do you?"

"I won't Frank, it's my new dress I bought from Morley's to replace the one you ruined. I bought it to wear to the christening, I wanted you to see it. I have a matching hat too. What do you think of it?"

"Yes, very nice. It just seems a wasted opportunity when there's no one around, that's all. I have to check the stables anyway."

"Well, we'll meet up later today. What are you wearing to see Mr Hooper? Do you want some potted beef on toast or some soup?"

"Both, please. I've discussed the kitchen with Jack, he's making it longer and there'll be a rest room next to it with a store room above. Do you think we should have a bath in the kitchen while we are altering it."

"If we can afford it it would be wonderful, but I'm worried about the cost. There is going to be so much to pay for."

"Let me see Mr Hooper, we'll know a bit more when I've been there."

"Have you seen to the stables?"

"No, I'll go now, it will be good to have a carriage here."

With that Frank disappeared downstairs. Florence, relieved, tried her hat and was very pleased; a good choice, she thought. Changing her dress, she went to see how Ann was. Still sleeping – good. Annie would be back with the shopping very soon. She went to the kitchen and made herself a cup of tea, and then the back door bumped and clattered open to reveal the bags of shopping and an ill-looking Annie.

"Cup of tea?" said Florence. "By the look of it you need one. Did you manage, were you sick today?"

"No Mrs Ginns, though I felt sick all morning, still do. I bought everything you need."

"Have your tea before you put it all away. I'm going to meet my parents this afternoon, so there'll be enough help on Sunday morning I'm sure. Will you and Mrs Disley be at All Saints? I hope you will."

"Mrs Disley is still ill, Mrs Ginns, they don't seem to know what's wrong with her, Walter is doing all he can, but having young Walter, he has his hands full."

"I knew she wasn't very well a while ago, didn't know she hadn't recovered, poor lady."

Frank came back then. "I have to go over to Battens', I need to get some hay and some straw, and a hay bag" he said.

"I'll have to get Ann ready, then when we've eaten get on our way."

She decided to go down High Street to get to St Margaret's. She was looking forward to the weekend, to putting Ann in her new cot and seeing Penny and Agnes again. Leicester was busy, but it was a Friday, so that was only to be expected. At the Clock Tower she turned into Churchgate. Time was getting on and she had to hurry, but she loved the hustle and bustle of St Margaret's.

She arrived only a few moments before her parents. She was surprised to see her father wearing a bowler hat.

"Lovely to see you again, and you have a new hat father, very modern!"

"Lovely to see you both too, let me see Ann, she's grown. I can see the cradle will be put to good use immediately.

"Jack Johnson has been over quite a lot, he's made a lovely job of it." "Jack seems to have been busy elsewhere, Annie is having a baby too. Shall we go? Let's go along Northgate Street, then up Highcross Street."

Kate took the pram from Florence, who carried her mother's bags.

"Frank should be home when we get there" said Florence. "He has been to see someone about a mortgage at the Westminster Bank. Ann will need feeding and so will we.

Mother will show you your bedroom Father, you can leave your hats and gloves in the hall."

They walked contentedly up Highcross Street, looking at All Saints as they walked past, Florence looking a little harder than the others maybe. As they crossed to go into number 98, her parents were glad to see signs of work being done to join the two houses together. Kate was pleased to see most of the rubbish had been moved, as it would be easier to push the pram to the front door. Frank was back, standing looking at the kitchen. He turned as he heard the door open.

"Hello, did you have a good journey? Would you like a drink? I'm sure Florence will make you some tea."

"I'll make the tea" said Kate. "Florence is going upstairs to feed and change Ann, she won't be too long." Kate wondered if he had held the baby yet and thought it unlikely.

After a while Florence came down the front stairs carrying Ann and they joined the others in the sitting room. Kate had found some biscuits and they were all drinking tea and munching them. All seemed calm.

"While we are all here," said Florence's father, "we'd like to pay for the cot. You will love it when you see it, Jack' s done a wonderful job."

"And we have brought you my old christening dress and hat, I can't believe I fitted into it once!" Kate gave the dress to Florence. It was made of fine cotton, almost transparent, and close to the bottom there were squares of Nottingham lace, which also decorated the little hat. The hat had a ribbon to tie it on, under the chin.

"Mother, it's beautiful!" said Florence. "I didn't know what to dress Ann in, but this will be perfect. Thank you."

"It will give me joy to see it used again."

"Aren't we lucky Frank?"

"We are indeed, thank you" said Frank.

"Are you ready for dinner? You must be hungry by now, biscuits or not. Mother, will you look after Ann whilst I go and cook?"

After they had eaten Florence took Ann up to bed, Kate washed up and the men went for a walk around the yard. When they all met up again, Frank looked over at Arthur and suggested they went out for a drink later.

"It will be a busy day tomorrow, we need an early night tonight" said Arthur. "He knew from Belgrave that Frank liked his booze, and thought he wouldn't want to leave the pub until as late as he could."

"How are things, Flo?" asked Kate.

"Just the same, I just let him do as he pleases. He still hasn't held Ann, which has upset me a lot. What can I do? I know he wanted a boy, perhaps next time. He has bought lots of bottles of champagne for tomorrow, far more than we can afford or will drink. He says some of his shooting friends are coming and that they like a drink."

"Oh dear, Flo. I told your father, it didn't seem a shock to him, he's known him all his life, as we have, and has seen him from the other side of the bar, remember."

"I know, Mother. He isn't well but he won't go to see the doctor. What am I going to do?"

After a while they decided they would have an early night,

even if the men didn't. Florence decided she would ask her mother if she would like to see Ann in her drawer for the last time, and Kate went through to the back bedroom. Florence told her mother she would wake them both in the morning; they were both in bed by 9.30.

CHAPTER FOUR

Thankfully Frank, maybe realising what a special day today was going to be, didn't wake Florence, and she woke only once to feed Ann. Putting on her work clothes, she woke Frank and went through Ann's room to wake her parents. Ann was just stirring, so Florence fed and dressed her, telling her today was a special day and she was going to see all four grandparents, her Uncle Francis and her two aunties, Penny and Agnes, and that she was going to church, the church where she had been held by Mr Gutteridge. Today she would have special water poured over her head, and she would be named Ann forever and ever.

Florence took Ann downstairs, where everyone was up. Frank had once again gone to check all was ready in the stables; how many more times, Florence wondered. She was happy to see her mother had made the tea.

"I'll just go and get the bacon and eggs from the cellar" she said. "Could you help Father please, there is quite a lot to bring up." Florence handed Ann to Kate and went to the cellar, clutching a box of matches to light the lanterns, suddenly remembering there was a basket she could use under the front stairs. Leaving her father lighting the lanterns, she went to fetch it.

In the meat safe was the bacon and fresh eggs; luckily Annie had hard boiled some eggs, but she hadn't shelled them, so the yolks would all be black. They loaded the basket with all that they would need, handed it to her father, then climbed back up as fast as she could. She hated it down there.

Things had changed since they had been in the cellar. Frank was back from the stables but had gone out again as his mother and father had arrived and was helping his father park the carriage and showing him where in the stables was best for the horse.

Florence was eager to see the cake her mother had made.

"Oh my goodness! With all the early morning rush we forgot it" said Kate. "We put it in the cradle last night."

Florence felt tears starting up; her mother had made it especially for today, especially for Ann.

"Don't cry Florence, I'm sorry."

"I'll be all right, I am just sad because you made it specially for Ann for today, but is too late now, it's Sunday, all the shops are closed. Maybe, if we have enough ingredients… no, I couldn't ask anyone now. Let's have some breakfast, then we can prepare the food for this afternoon."

Everyone was in the sitting room, as there wasn't enough room in the kitchen. Then the front door opened, pushed by Frank, who was walking in backwards carrying the cradle. He put it on the table.

"Oh my goodness it's beautiful, look Ann, it's your new bed! No more drawer for you, you're a big girl now. Isn't it wonderfully well made! Frank, will you take it upstairs soon, I will put Ann in it whilst we have breakfast."

Just at that moment another carriage appeared outside the window. Everyone looked at each other – who could it be? It stopped directly outside and Frank went out to see; there was the sound of laughter and conversation. Everyone inside strained to hear who it was. After a few minutes a very happy Frank and his brother came into the sitting room. With a broad smile Frank said, "The carriage has been lent to us by my parents. The cake your mother made for today is inside it, Florence."

"Honestly?"

"Yes, honestly."

"What a wonderful day this is turning out to be!"

"But it won't be unless we have breakfast soon, Florence" said Frank petulantly. Kate said she would cook bacon and eggs for all if Florence found another frying pan. Frank and his father carried the cot to Ann's room, where Florence made up the cot and put Ann into it. She cried as it was new to her after all, but John had made it so well.

After they'd finished breakfast, they all went to do various jobs. Kate and Mrs Ginns senior washed up and tidied the kitchen, and Florence went to see if the 'office' was ready. She carried the cake in and put it on a table in the centre of the window. All she needed to do now was get the champagne glasses out and tea cups and saucers and put them on a tablecloth in the sitting room.

The two mothers had covered the table with bread rolls with ham, egg, cucumber and salmon; all looked very appetising. Then the tea cups were put out. The rolls were put onto plates and covered with tea towels, then put to cool.

Florence dressed Ann in her dress again. It was so much more elegant than her own outfit. Then she dressed herself, with her mother's help. The fabric was still a bit stiff. She put on her hat, secured it with a hat pin, picked up her shawl and gloves and was ready. She picked up Ann from her new cot and went to join the others. All thought how lovely her outfit was, so that made her happy.

Frank ran in; he'd been looking over the carriage and had lost track of the time. He shot upstairs to wash and change. When he came down they all went out and walked to All Saints, Ann being carried by her mother. Several people were standing outside in the sun.

Agnes and Penny were standing near the font. Florence looked around and saw Annie Johnson and Jack, her husband. William Gutteridge was also there.

The Rev Swingler came out from the vestry and asked who the godparents were. He asked them to come to the font, which already had the water in it. The godparents all agreed to support Ann. Water was put over her head and the Reverend put a cross on her forehead; now she was part of God's family.

When the prayers had finished Ann was handed to Agnes to carry her home. The vicar went outside and poured the water into the ground - it had been blessed for Ann, no one else.

The ceremony over, everyone who had attended walked up to number 98 except the Johnsons, who peeled off to go home to Friars Causeway.

Back home, Florence immediately put the water on to boil and Mrs Ginns went to put the food out. Ann was being handed around the ladies, whilst some of the men went to have a look at the new premises. Most agreed that a roof over the carriages would be a wonderful idea. When they went back into the house tea was made, sandwiches were eaten, presents opened and conversation was jovial and convivial. The vicar came for a cup of tea but didn't stay long.

Eventually Frank decided he would fetch the champagne from the cellar. Florence told him she'd left the matches by the lanterns, so down he went. After a few moments there was the sound of breaking glass and a sickening thud, then silence.

The conversation abruptly stopped. The nearest to the cellar door was William Gutteridge, who looked down the stairs and called for help. Frank was lying on the stairs at a very strange angle. He was unconscious and blood was flowing from his head.

"Can someone get down below him?" Said William. "It will be a squeeze. Then we need to get him up and straight in the hall. Can someone get something to stem the blood, and someone go for the doctor?"

"I had better do that" said Florence, "No one knows where he is but you and me."

"I need someone strong to help here, and mind the broken glass won't you."

Steve and Dick, Frank's shooting friends, Frank's father and Francis managed to haul Frank up to the hall. The women brought clean towels to bandage him. When everything had been done all stood around in stunned silence, looking down at Frank and his bandaged head.

Just as Dr Angus and William arrived, a noise came from Frank. He was waking up. Dr Angus knelt down to examine him, looking into his eyes. Frank asked for some water. Dr Angus asked him if he had any pain anywhere. Frank said that he just felt weak. The doctor then asked if he could sit up; he couldn't, so the men were asked to carry him upstairs to the bed.

Ann was being cared for by Penny and Agnes while all the drama was going on, but now she began to cry. Florence was surprised she had lasted as long as she had. Now Florence had to excuse herself and went up the back stairs to feed and change Ann in her bedroom. She could hear them carrying Frank up the front stairs, but at the moment she was too busy with Ann. She was comforted by hearing the doctor saying "Today, Mr Ginns, you will have a pain in your head, and feel weak. You lost consciousness from what Mr Gutteridge says, for about five minutes. I would like you to stay in bed until I call again on Tuesday. For now though, rest. I know you have a lot to do, but you must rest for now."

Kate Cambers appeared with a cup of tea, to say that guests were leaving and that no one had fancied the cake in the circumstances. She understood.

Kate offered to stay, but Florence said it was not necessary. Having changed Ann she handed her over to her mother and crossed the landing to see Frank, who was looking very drowsy. Dr Angus said he had just given him morphine for his pain, so he would sleep now until the morning.

Florence went down to the office to find Penny, Agnes William, Francis and both sets of parents waiting for news.

"Well, the doctor is coming to see him again on Tuesday" she told them. "He has given him morphine for the pain and says he must rest, even though he knows that he has a lot to do. William, as Dr Angus knows you better than anyone else could I please ask you to show the doctor out? Use the door facing the bottom of the stairs, there's a key in the lock."

"My pleasure, Florence" smiled William. All four parents noticed the warmth between the two.

"Mother, I know I said I said I didn't want you to stay, but thinking about it, please will you stay for another couple of days? Father, will you be all right until Wednesday, when the doctor has been?"

"I'll manage, might have to get the godparents to give me some help though." He smiled at the girls and Francis.

"What am I to do with the bandage? Should I just leave it where it is until the doctor has been?"

"I think I would, Florence" said Frank Ginns senior.

"I am sure when he wakes tomorrow he will be much better" said Kate. "Leave it until the doctor sees it again on Wednesday."

"I'd try to make Frank to resist removing it, the doctor will do what needs to be done on Tuesday."

William asked if he could be of any help with Frank's toilet needs. Kate and Florence looked relieved. It was not something they had thought about, but a man seemed a good idea. They hoped Frank would be able to walk when he woke tomorrow.

"How are you girls getting back?" asked Frank.

"We must leave soon to get the bus" sighed Penny.

"We can all go in our carriage" Frank's father said, so it was agreed.

"Don't leave your hat behind, Father, it's in the hall, remember."

"I'll leave my wife behind before I leave my hat" joked Arthur. "Mother and I will start to clear everything away when you have left. Maybe you can take some cake back with you, what a shame it finished the way it did. I had better go and see if Frank's all right."

"I must leave you, Florence. I'll call in tomorrow" said William.

"Thank you for all your help, it will be good to see you tomorrow. Mother and I will do all we can, but thank you."

Francis went to harness the carriage, brought it up to the door and waited. His father was going to sit alongside him. The two godmothers climbed into the carriage, followed by Arthur.

"See you all very soon ladies. I'll write if Frank's recovery changes anything. Thank you too, for Ann's presents."

With that they were gone, trotting up Highcross Street. Florence went up to see Frank, who was sleeping quietly. Then she looked in at Ann, who was also sleeping. She would need feeding and changing before long. Until then she would go and help her mother.

The first thing she thought of doing was cleaning the cellar steps, but someone had already cleared them of broken glass and wiped up the splashes of champagne and blood. "I don't know who cleaned the steps" said Florence to her mother. "I was just about to do them myself."

"I have no idea" said Kate. "At least Annie won't have to clear them tomorrow. It will be a shock for Charlie and the builders when they hear what's happened. I'll go and wash the rest and bring them through, and another tea towel, if there is one, they were all used for poor Frank's head weren't they?"

"Yes, someone has put them to soak in a bucket of cold water, again I don't know who."

"Who were the two men who helped carry him upstairs? I didn't know either of them, though your pa thinks he's seen them before at Belgrave."

"Oh they were friends of Frank, he goes shooting with them and they'd probably come to talk about next season's dates and to drink Ann's champagne. Neither happened, did it?"

Florence had forgotten when she was meeting Penny; she'd have to check her diary. She then went across to see Frank, who was still lying in the same position. He looked so yellow. Surely the doctor had noticed? It would have to be discussed on Tuesday.

All Florence wanted now was to sleep. She kissed her mother, then went up the back stairs so she could see Ann as she went through her bedroom. The nights were drawing in quickly now, and it was almost dark. Ann seemed to sleep more soundly in Jack Johnson's cradle. As soon as Frank was better she would go and thank him.

Still no snoring from Frank; he was still where he had been laid. Florence touched him. He was clammy but still breathing shallowly. Florence undressed and lay beside her husband, relieved in a way that for once he was so undemanding. Then she slept.

Ann woke her once during the night. On her way back to bed after feeding her Florence was pleased to see that Frank had changed position and when she felt his forehead he felt cooler; more normal.

Charlie arrived at seven o'clock, waking Florence. She knew what he would be doing this morning, so she just lay and looked at Frank, who, apart from his bandage, looked a bit more himself; still so yellow though. She could hear Highcross Street slowly coming alive, the sparrows chirruping, the clomping of horses, doors banging and odd snatches of conversation, then the sound builders arriving. It was no good, she'd have to get up and let them in and start the day.

Ann was her priority, once she'd dressed. Ann was just waking, so Florence fed her and changed her. It seemed to be quicker each time she did it. Working clothes today, much easier she thought. Once Ann was winded she took her to her mother, then went to see Frank, who was slowly waking. His first words were "I need some water, I am so thirsty. What happened?"

Florence gave him a small glass of water, which was gone in seconds.

"I will tell you what happened as soon as I've seen Charlie and Mother and made you breakfast and seen the builders. Mother will bring you breakfast while I do everything else. Won't be long."

Florence found her mother and Ann cocooned together in bed.

"Frank has woken. I have to get Charlie to sort out the horse. He can go over to Batten's and buy what he needs, water it, muck the stables out, I expect. Would you get Frank some breakfast and some tea Ma?"

Florence found Charlie clearing up after the party.

"Good morning Charlie, I thought you would be here. Things didn't go to plan yesterday. In fact Mr Ginns is upstairs in bed with an injury. We now have a horse and a carriage. Please will you go down to the stables and see what you can do down there and see what we need to buy from Batten's."

"Mrs Ginns, what on earth has happened to Mr Ginns?"

Florence was half way through telling the story when William arrived.

"Good morning to you both" he said. "Will it be all right if I go up, Florence? I am in a rush, but sure Frank may need help."

"Do, William, my mother is up there too. Frank was half asleep when I saw him last. I will be up soon, I don't know if he can walk yet."

"Don't worry, I am sure your mother and I can find out, I'll call you if I need you."

"I will be up soon and thank you for coming."

Florence then turned back to Charlie. "Can you do that for us Charlie? Let me know if you need some money for Batten's won't you?"

"Of course I will. I suppose it ruined your day?"

"It did rather."

Some of the builders looked agitated. They wanted to be working and were standing around waiting for someone to let them in.

"I am so sorry to have had to keep you waiting" said Florence. "We have had a crisis. Please remember Mr Ginns is ill in bed in the next room. I'll go and let you in."

She unlocked the door at the bottom of the front stairs and the builders almost pushed her away. William stood with Frank, talking quietly. Frank was sitting up now which, to Flo's untrained eye, looked promising.

"Florence, glad you're here. Thank heavens Frank managed to walk a few steps, which was all he needed."

"Thank you William, for today, and from what you've said for yesterday too."

"My pleasure. I must go, until the doctor has seen you. Rest, Frank."

The builders could be heard in the room next to Frank, loudly trying to be quiet.

"Did Mother make your breakfast?"

"William arrived before it was ready, only wanted a boiled egg. Some tea would be good too, I'm really thirsty."

"So you know what happened yesterday then?"

"Yes, I can't remember it at all."

"The doctor is coming to see you tomorrow, has anyone told you? He says you must rest until he sees you."

"I'd like to take my bandage off, it's itching, what do you think Flo?"

"I would leave it until the doctor comes tomorrow. How much do you think he will cost?"

"Well, I was an emergency, on a Sunday, so it'll be expensive I expect."

"I'm sure."

"I'm just going down to see what mother is doing with your egg. Do you want a *Farmers' Weekly* to read? You don't want to see the builders, do you? They're just beginning to re plaster the walls, so they aren't making too much noise, just a lot of dust."

Florence wondered what her Ma had done with Ann. She went down the back stairs and opened the door at the bottom to an empty sitting room. Climbing down, she looked out of the window to see her mother and Annie Johnson both looking lovingly into the pram. No wonder Frank still hadn't had his egg and tea.

Florence tapped on the window. They both saw her and came scurrying in through the back door.

"Good Morning Mrs Ginns, I'm sorry, I was distracted by Ann. I hear the christening ended badly."

"Good morning Annie, it was lovely to see you and John in church yesterday. Yes, things went wrong when we were home. Mr Ginns is still in bed, which is where he will stay until the doctor has seen him tomorrow. Mother, please make Frank's breakfast and a cup of tea, in fact if you could make us all one. I suppose the egg cups turned up then Annie?"

"They were in the boxes, as you said, in the 'office'."

"Jack's crib, oh Annie it is delightful, even Ann seems to like it, she sleeps so well. I will call round to thank him when things have settled here. I don't think Mr Ginns is too bad. Where are the egg cups, Annie? I only need one."

"I put them on a shelf under the front stairs, I'll go and get one for you."

"The bridge between the houses is coming on fast, they are plastering at the moment. It's going to be a larger room than the sitting room by far."

"When are they putting the upstairs toilet in? Soon I hope."

"William was able to help this morning, do you think he will call again this evening? Perhaps Frank will be better to walk to the toilet downstairs. He has a gazunder, but he may need the toilet."

"This is a bit embarrassing, isn't it?" said Florence. "Annie, please would you talk to Charlie? He's sorting the stable out at the moment, to get the office clean and tidy again. The cake, if it's still there, can be cut, and you and John might like a piece each. I'm going to see Frank and collect his breakfast things. I'm sure Charlie will be with you soon."

Florence walked up the front stairs, feeling happy and excited that at long last, Frank and the doctor would finally meet up, she hoped. When she walked into the bedroom, her mother had closed the door to keep the plaster dust out. Frank was reading *Farmers' Weekly* and his breakfast lay eaten. Only an empty eggshell remained and crumbs of toast.

"Do you feel any better now you've eaten?" she asked.

"I still have a headache, I really want the bandage off Florence, it's getting more and more itchy."

"I've told you, wait until tomorrow, it's only a few hours to go. Did William say whether he will call again tonight?"

"He said he would, but I've told you, there's no need."

"Well, I'm glad he is, I think he's coming for my benefit, as much as yours. Your mother goes home tomorrow, remember."

"What's happening out there?"

"Ann's in her pram outside, Charlie is dealing with the stable, going over to Battens' this morning to get anything vital. Annie is helping Charlie return the office to the way we want it. And the builders are plastering next door. I haven't had time to go outside yet."

"I'm sure when the doctor has checked me over tomorrow we can press on with things."

"I'm going downstairs. Is there anything you want?"

"I'd really like a cigarette and a drink."

"I'll bring you a cup of coffee, but no cigarettes in bed."

He hadn't mentioned cigarettes for a while. She thought he must be feeling better.

William arrived around six and escorted Frank to the downstairs toilet, noting that his walking looked back to normal.

"You look back to your old self, thank heavens, but it will be good to see the doctor tomorrow" he said.

"Yes I know, but I feel fine now, apart from this damn bandage."

Before long Frank was back in bed and William had left, saying that he could see Frank was able to cope and wishing him well with the doctor tomorrow. It had quietened down now; Ann had been fed and changed and Annie Johnson and Charlie had left, both with large slices of christening cake. Annie had another piece for Ellen Disley, who was no better. The doctor had finally been to see her but they couldn't afford to pay for him again. Only the builders remained, and they would be gone soon.

Frank was beginning to feel tired and fell into bed. Florence and Kate sat reading in the sitting room; they heard the builders go and peace reigned.

CHAPTER FIVE

The following morning the rain was falling in sheets; there was no wind at all. The sky was gunmetal grey and the clouds were different tones, some almost black. The rain kept coming.

Frank was worried when he saw the weather. His carriage! But Charlie had checked it. Frank knew then that a cover needed to be erected over the yard. Kate had been asked by Florence to unlock the door at the bottom of the stairs for the builders. Outside work would be interrupted, but the plastering should be finished today. Frank thought perhaps if it stopped raining they could open the windows and carry on outside, but there was nothing to do until the doctor arrived.

Florence brought him coffee at eleven and told him the rain was stopping slowly, Annie and Charlie were there and she had paid Charlie for whatever he had needed to buy at Batten's. Frank had read and re-read *Farmers' Weekly* and was in possession of all the prices of every farm animal and especially horses; he would be buying soon.

Florence came up again and made sure he'd had a wash and

changed his pyjamas. When the doctor arrived, Florence brought him upstairs.

"How are you now?" he asked Frank. "You're looking much better than you did on Sunday."

"I'm feeling much better, but please will you take the bandage off? It is itching so much."

"First things first Mr Ginns, let me take your blood pressure."

Florence stood at the end of the bed whilst he did this, and then slowly and carefully removed the bandage. Some blood had dried and was harder to separate away, but finally, gloriously, it was off.

"You are very yellow Mr Ginns, do you drink very much alcohol?"

"Tell him the truth Frank, or I will" said Florence in a low voice.

"Well, I do like to have a drink at the pub at the end of the day."

"I see. Well now I've seen you I would like you to go for some tests to The Royal Infirmary as soon as possible and come up the road and see me a week after, when your results should be with me. More important than anything, you need to stop drinking. How old are you?"

"Twenty-eight."

"Well the sooner you get to the infirmary the better it will be."

Doctor Angus left after telling Frank he could get up but take it easy for a while, reminding him that he had been knocked out. Frank asked how much he would be charging. Doctor Angus told them, and Frank said he would bring the money over within the next couple of days. With that Florence showed the doctor out.

When she returned Frank was getting dressed.

"Well, it sounds serious" she said. "When shall we go to the hospital?"

"Oh don't panic, he told me to stop drinking, I'll not drink as much. You never told me you'd been to see him. When was that?"

"It was after you tore my dress. I told him your attitude changed after you had had a drink or two, and that you forced yourself on me, even though Ann was only days old. But it was more than that, Frank, he didn't like the look of you, your colour. You're getting yellower, you know that don't you? Perhaps it's your liver, or maybe your kidneys, I don't know, I'm not a doctor."

With that Florence gathered up her skirt and went down to see what was happening downstairs. Her mother was pleased to see her and enquired what the doctor had said. Florence told her that it was serious and the doctor wanted Frank to go to hospital for tests.

"It's his liver, that's why he is so yellow" said Kate. "His eyes have gone yellow too, and he is tired a lot. It definitely seems to me to be his liver, Flo. What is he going to do about it?"

"Doctor Angus has told him to stop drinking, he has said to me he will drink less. He won't though, you'll see. You're probably right, he doesn't seem to be worried."

"Oh Florence, do you want me to stay? Can I do anything?"

"No Mother, you must go home. When does your bus go?"

"Half past three. I haven't any packing. I will strip the bed but I have nothing else to do."

"I feel I should stay here with Frank, hope you understand."

"You must go to the hospital with him. You will, won't you?" said Kate.

"Of course I will, but tests and results won't change Frank, you know that as well as I do."

Annie came into the sitting room. She was about to go, and only had to put her overall behind the kitchen door.

"I'm glad Mr Ginns is feeling well enough to be up" she said. "He was in the office as I came through. Charlie went about an hour ago, we've put the office back to how it was, Mr Ginns was pleased with it I think."

"What's he doing now, do you know?"

"He's just going to see what Charlie has done with the horse. I should know its name, Drambuie I think, I can't remember, Mr Ginns did say. And to look at the carriage now the rain has stopped."

"It was a real downpour, wasn't it? Mother is going home this afternoon, so you won't see her for a while."

"Goodbye Mrs Cambers, see you again soon, I hope."

"Goodbye Annie, I hope all goes well with your pregnancy, I'm sure we will see you before it's born."

"William was able to help this morning, do you think he'll call again this evening? Perhaps Frank will be better to walk to the toilet downstairs. Annie, please would you talk to Charlie, who is sorting the stable out? We need to get the office clean and tidy again. The cake, if it is still there, can be cut and you and John may like a piece each. I'm going to see Frank and collect his breakfast things. I'm sure Charlie will be with you soon."

Florence was glad she had Annie to talk to when there was no one else around. She looked to be thickening around her waist now and her sickness seemed to have ended. What was she going to do when she stopped working? Would she come back when she became a mother? She decided there and then that she would ask her tomorrow. Annie hung up her overall and left.

"I'll just see if Frank would like tea with us before you go, Mother."

"I'll make it, you go and see him."

Florence walked down the yard. Everything was covered with drips of water and some fell on her. Everywhere smelt fresh and sweet, she thought as she walked into the gloom of the stables.

"How's Drambuie? How are you? I've come to ask you to come up and have a cup of tea with us before mother goes, very soon."

"I could do with a drink, though Charlie's done a good job I still need to muck out and tidy up more, but I'll come up and wash first. You are wet, why? It's not raining now."

"It was just drips, that's all. Obviously I walked past the carriage. You do need cover down there, I agree. How much will it cost do you think?"

"I'll get Jack Harrison to give me a quote."

Florence gathered up her skirt and walked back to the house. Her skirt was damp too, she noticed.

"He's coming up for tea, I think he's doing too much though."

Frank came in through the back door and grunted to Kate while washing, then slumped down in his chair, obviously waiting for his tea. Kate and Florence looked at each other but said nothing. They drank their tea, then noticed Frank had gone to sleep. Florence quietly asked her mother if there was anything she needed to take with her back to Belgrave. All she wanted to do was see Ann, who was now back in her cradle. When she had looked at her she came down the front stairs not wanting to wake Frank.

"He's still not well, you take care of yourself" said Kate.

"Don't worry mother, I will."

Soon the door quietly closed and Florence was alone with her thoughts and a sleeping Frank.

CHAPTER SIX

Frank never did go to the hospital. He said he felt well enough and would drink less, but six months went by and nothing changed. He still forced himself on Florence when he'd had too much to drink. Florence hated it.

And then she found she was pregnant again. When she told Frank, all he said was "Let's hope it's a real baby, a boy this time."

Florence had been right all the time. That was why he had never held Ann, not like Mr Gutteridge, who had held her willingly and readily.

Annie Johnson gave birth to a boy. She told Mrs Ginns that apart from feeding him, her mother said she would look after him, and she would be back at work as soon as she could, which she was. Mrs Disley was getting worse. They thought she had had a bout of bronchitis which had turned to pneumonia, but they could no longer afford the doctor. Walter was at his wits' end.

Jack Johnson, being a close neighbour, suggested that Walter should go over to see Mr Ginns, as he was about the same age as himself and just getting started and might need help. Walter made up his mind he would go and see Mr Ginns the next morning while his wife and son were sleeping.

After he had organised Walter Junior (they had been calling him 'Wal' so they wouldn't get them confused), he helped Ellen, gave her breakfast and told her he was going round to see Mr Ginns whilst the two of them had a sleep later that morning.

"I want to see if there's maybe work there for me" he said. "I need to get some money, then we can get a doctor to make you fit again. It was Jack Johnson's suggestion really."

"Thank heavens someone is thinking" sighed Ellen.

Once everything was done Walter put the pair of them to bed and walked around to find Frank Ginns, who was looking at the almost completed front of number 98.

"Good morning Mr Ginns, I live in one of your cottages on Friars Causeway, my wife was one of the ladies who helped Mrs Ginns when she had your daughter" he began. "Unfortunately she is now ill. I am looking after her and my two-year-old son. The reason I am here is to see if you have any work that I can do. I need money for the doctor you see."

"What type of work can you do? I need a man who can turn his hand to anything at the moment, when can you start?"

"I must get someone to look after Ellen, my wife, and my son. Can I have two or three days? And what do you pay?"

Frank told him what he was prepared to pay him for a trial for a month, then they would renegotiate. It was agreed. Walter left to find someone to look after Ellen and young Wal. Maybe his mother would do it, she only lived on Bath Lane. He'd go and see her that afternoon, but now he must go back to Friars Causeway; they were both still asleep, he was relieved.

Wal woke first. Walter could tell he needed changing; he'd become an old hand at looking after him in the last few months. Then Ellen woke with a bad bout of coughing. Walter left Wal sitting on the wooden floor near his cot, playing with some blocks of wood. Walter knew the cot was too small for him now, but there hadn't been time to get a new one since Ellen had become ill.

Walter hurried in to get his wife some water, and slowly her coughing quietened.

"That wasn't very pleasant for either of us, was it?" he said. "I have news for you which may make you feel a bit better. I have a job at Mr Ginns' trial for a month, maybe longer."

A croaky "That's wonderful news". Then the coughing began again, worse than before.

"We can get a doctor to see you then" Walter said when the coughing stopped at last. "I'll get you another glass of water. Do you want anything to eat? I'm getting Wal something, he's sitting by his cot. I'll take him down with me, shall I?"

"Bring him here, I haven't seen him much for a while."

Walter took Wal in to his mother. He was playing happily with a wooden Noah's Ark. Probably the sound of the wooden animals clattering against the wooden hull had kept him quiet. Walter stood at the narrow door and told him his mummy would like to see him. Wal really didn't want to stop playing, but Walter scooped him up and carried him in to Ellen, putting him beside her on the bed.

"I'll go and get you both something to eat, then I'll take Wal to Bath Lane" he said. Ellen thought, not for the first time, what a kind man he was. This illness hadn't been part of their plans when they had married. "In sickness and in health", said so glibly at the time, seemed so important now.

Ellen had yet another coughing fit, which scared Wal and he began to cry. Ellen tried to placate him, while Walter rushed upstairs and grabbed him quickly from the bed.

"Mother is poorly Wal, that is why she has to stay in bed all the time, but soon the doctor will see her and make her better. Let's go downstairs and have our food and leave your mother to rest."

Having eaten, Walter went upstairs again to see if Ellen needed anything before he went to Bath Lane, telling her he would tell Mrs Johnson and she might check her at some point; they had become friends since Ann's birth. It only took ten minutes to walk there, mainly downhill towards the river. Bath Lane was so called because of the public baths there, the only place many could have a bath with hot water, literally, on tap.

Walter's mother was surprised and delighted to see them both.

"Would you like a cup of tea? A juice for you, Wal? Why are you here? There's something wrong, is it Ellen?"

"Well it is and it isn't, Ma. She is no better, coughing so much she can't breathe very easily, that's why I've had to find some work. I've found a job as an odd job man, I'll be working for Mr Ginns but I have to find someone to look after Ellen and Wal whilst I am at work, then we can afford a doctor to see her. Can you help, Mother please? It won't be for too long, I don't think, but you will have to come to Friars Causeway, obviously."

"Oh Walter, I thought when I saw you both that something had happened to Ellen. Of course I'll come, the poor girl needs all the help we can give her. And it's been hard for you to cope too."

"Thank you Mother, I'll go and tell Mr Ginns and Ellen too. Will you begin on Monday? I expect I'll have to be there at eight, is that all right?"

"I'll be up by then, then Wal and I will look after his mummy, won't we Wal?" The little boy smiled.

"Thank you mother, I've left her alone, so I'd better go."

Taking Wal's hand, he walked back up the gentle hill to Friars Causeway, going into the darkness of the passageway between two of the small houses, for that was what they were, Walter thought. By now he was having to carry Wal, who was too tired to walk.

"We're back" Walter called from the kitchen. He put the kettle on the stove to make some tea to take to Ellen. There was no sound from upstairs but that of laboured breathing. The fireguard was in place, but the fire was out, so he left Wal where he was, playing on the scrap mat Ellie had made when she was pregnant. With a cup and saucer in each hand he climbed the steep stairs to see how his wife was. Her breathing sounded worse than ever.

He put her tea down as quietly as he could on the small rattan and bamboo bedside table, but she roused, so he sat down on the buttoned green velvet chair; Mrs Johnson must have been and put all the papers on the floor.

"Hello dear, I see Mrs Johnson came to see you whilst I was at Mother's."

After another coughing fit she said, almost whispering now, "How did you get on?"

"Drink your tea first. I'll get the doctor to come and see you next week so I can go to work, by the sound of you he can't come soon enough."

Walter drank his tea, noticing Ellen hadn't touched hers.

"Drink your tea dear, whilst it is hot."

"Don't fuss, I'll drink it when I want."

"I just think it would be better for you, for your chest, if you drank it hot. That's all. I'm going to fetch Wal up, won't be long."

The next morning, after Walter had fed, changed and washed the two of them, he again asked Mrs Johnson if she could pop in while her son was sleeping. All this was organised and Walter went along Friars Causeway and up Highcross Street, turning into number 98. There wasn't a sign of Mr Ginns. He rang the front door bell, which was answered by a shortish, rounded lady wearing an apron.

"Good morning, my name Is Walter Disley, I'm looking for Mr Ginns."

"Good morning" said Annie. "Mr Ginns is down in the stables, I think, do go down the yard. I'm sure you'll find him down there."

"Thank you."

Walter walked Into the darkness to find Frank in the middle of mucking out the lone horse.

"Good morning Mr Ginns, I will be doing that for you next week, I have someone to look after Ellen and Wal. I hope that pleases you."

"Hello Walter, yes it pleases me very much. For now you will have to use the same space as Charlie, our early morning help. He starts early in the morning, unlocks the doors, lights the fires, cleans all the shoes and cleans the offices he's a small bald man, very quiet.

"So I will meet him on Monday?"

"I won't see him before you come, you'll have to introduce yourself."

Once Walter had gone Frank realised how tired he was, which surprised him. He would go up to the house when he had finished, have a Drambuie and take a rest. The first thing he would want Walter to do was to paint the carriage in the subdued colours of The Great Central Railway; then he could use it as a cab and for funerals. Then he thought he needed to buy a black horse. He would check in *Farmers' Weekly* to see if there was one advertised for sale. He knew his father had a black horse, but he didn't want to keep asking him for help.

He had now walked back up the yard and went in through the back door to find Annie Johnson was in the kitchen. He asked her to make him tea, and sat in his chair to look at *Farmer's Weekly*. By the time Annie brought the tea through to him, he was asleep.

Florence came through; she had been cleaning the front office. The builders had just finished putting the black and white tiles down for the entrance to the business. She liked them, and thought they might make a good floor for the kitchen when, eventually, they had it enlarged.

Annie was still in the kitchen, folding up the washing she'd just pulled down from the frame above their heads where it had dried.

"Afternoon Mrs Ginns, how are you? I made Mr Ginns a cup of tea a while ago, but he was asleep when I took it to him. Maybe he'd like another, shall I go and ask him?"

"It was still there when I came by. He is still asleep. I will make him a fresh one when he wakes."

"Is he all right, Mrs Ginns? I haven't really seen him since I had John."

"How is John? You know I'm expecting don't you?" Florence said, changing the subject.

Having made tea for Mrs Ginns, Annie hung up her overall and left Mrs Ginns alone. Florence went back into the sitting room. Nothing had changed, and the tea was still untouched. Frank was still sitting there; he hadn't moved an inch.

Then she realised that she could see no sign of breathing. She put out a hand to touch his shoulder. He slumped forward, and she gasped in shock. Frank wasn't asleep. He was dead.

Florence felt many emotions at once; shock, sorrow and fear, but mainly relief. She turned from his body and stood looking absently out of the window. There was a heavy silence, and she felt a cold loneliness wrap itself around her. But tears did not come; they were still far away.

She made her mind to be strong, for her own sake and for Ann and the unborn one. What to do? She needed some help now. She needed Mrs Johnson. She'd have to take Ann with her and then go up to St Nicholas Street and find William Gutteridge. She went up, wrapped Ann in a blanket and walked around to Annie's, thinking how heavy she was becoming, or maybe it was because she was pregnant.

"No wonder Mr Ginns didn't drink your tea, Annie, I'm afraid he's passed away."

"Oh Mrs Ginns! I'm so sorry, what a shock! I can't believe it! What do you want Jack and me to do?"

"Can I leave Ann with you for a while? I need to go and find Mr Gutteridge, he will help me. Then someone will have to go to Belgrave to tell my parents and Frank's family."

"Oh please go, Mrs Ginns, we will do anything to help. I'm so shocked."

"So am I Annie. He refused to listen to Doctor Angus. I must go."

Florence ran up Highcross Street and turned into St Nicholas Street. She found Mr Hyde's jewellery shop and banged violently on the door, thinking as she did so that William wouldn't hear if he was upstairs. There must be a back way somewhere. She tried again with all her might. There was someone in the shop, but she couldn't see who it was - Mr Hyde?

It was William. At the sight of him tears began to flow. It was going to be all right, she wouldn't be alone any more.

William unlocked the door and Florence fell sobbing into his arms.

"What on earth is the matter?" he asked. "Why are you crying? Something's happened. Is it Ann or Frank?" But she could not speak. Her sobs became louder.

"Come inside" he said. Without letting her go he closed the door to the street and the nosy passers-by.

"Now, take a deep breath, stop crying, and tell me what's happened." He held her warmly in his arms.

"Oh William, it's Frank, he's dead. You were the first person I thought of. He's in his chair in the sitting room, what do I do?"

"Oh that's terrible news! We need to tell Doctor Angus first. When did Frank last see him?"

"Last week, he wanted him to go for some tests six months ago, but he was adamant, said he would drink less. He didn't of course. Doctor Angus was keeping his eye on him so he saw him frequently."

The doctor's was halfway between their homes. William took over, realising Florence had had a shock and wasn't in a fit state to go over it again yet. It was all a blur to Flo, except that she remembered the doctor using one of the new telephone. She had heard about them, but to see one being spoken into was hard to understand. The doctor was calling Earps', the local undertaker, just yards away, to ask them to take Mr Ginns to their premises. There was no need for the doctor to treat it as suspicious. But he had been only twenty-eight, and Florence was expecting another soon.

William and Florence walked back to number 98. Florence didn't want to go in, so they went to Annie's. William left her there and let himself in to await the Earps, who came very soon and took Frank back to their premises to lay him out.

Florence and Annie, in the meantime, went over the afternoon's events. Jack left them to talk and made them tea in the kitchen.

After about an hour, William appeared. When Florence saw him a feeling of relief flowed through her whole being, reminding her again that she wasn't alone any more.

"Earps' have taken Frank away" he said. "I said you would sort the arrangements with them tomorrow, I thought you would rather see them after you've had a sleep. I'll go with you if you'd like me to."

"I really would, yes please."

William carried Ann back home and opened the door for Florence.

"Are you all right to go in? I have tidied up a bit."

"Yes, I'll be fine, you did move the tea though, didn't you?"

"Oh Florence, your sense of humour is coming back, that's good. Let's go in, shall we?"

"Yes, I need to get Ann fed and to bed as soon as I can."

"Well, while you do that I'll find something to eat, shall I?"

"I really am not very hungry William, just get yourself something. Have a look in the cellar, the door is opposite the front door. There are matches and a candle on the shelf on the wall, so you can see your way. There's a meat safe with bacon and eggs."

William began to think he ought to stay with them tonight; presumably he could use the spare room. Despite her bravado an awful thing had happened and she must be in shock. He ought to stay – just for support, or that was what he told himself. He kept remembering how it had felt when to hold her earlier. She had been a sodden mess, but...

William cooked, with some difficulty, bacon and eggs, and when Florence came downstairs she sat at the table and ate.

"I was wondering if you would like me to stay here tonight" said William. "In the spare room, of course."

"Yes, I would like that very much" said Florence. She knew she needed him there; she knew she was falling love with him. Ever since they'd met in All Saints she'd known he was the one for her, but it was too soon, far too soon of course.

"We need to talk about the funeral arrangements" said William. "Do you want Earps' to do it or would you like my business to do it?"

"I didn't know you did funerals as well, I thought you were hauliers, that was all you did. But someone must go to Belgrave and tell them what's happened. Would you go for me, William?

You're well-spoken and I'm sure you're good with people in these circumstances. After we have finished at Earps' it would be lovely if you did the funeral, but you are supporting me so much. It would mean we'd have to move Frank, and honestly I can't. I hope you understand."

"Florence, you needn't worry about anything. I will organise it all."

"Oh William, thank heavens you're here."

"You look very tired. Look, you're pregnant and you've had a hard day, you should go to bed. I'll lock up and do everything down here. Who will be here tomorrow morning?"

"It's Saturday isn't it? Charlie won't be here, nor will Annie, so no one. What time do we need to go to Earps'?"

"Don't worry I will go and sort it."

"Thank you so much. I will see you about eight in the morning then. You'll find everything you need up there. Do take some water up, that's all you'll need I think. Goodnight William."

"Goodnight Florence, I really hope you sleep well."

It took Florence a while to settle down and sleep. At least Ann now slept through the night, though she still woke early. Florence woke the next morning not knowing whether it was the baby inside kicking or her aching back, but then, like a ton of bricks falling around her, she remembered. Frank was dead. She knew she should feel sad, but she felt relief. He had been a rapist and a drunkard. Everything would be better now, she felt, maybe not straight away, there was a lot to do, but in time. Her star sign was Aries and she wouldn't let anything break her. And William seemed to want to care, to support her as much as he could.

Ann was bawling now, and she went and fed her, thinking that soon she would need a bigger bed, especially with the new baby coming soon. Laying Ann on the bed in her bedroom, she hurriedly dressed and went downstairs. William was standing in the kitchen with a cup of tea in his hands.

"How did you sleep?" he asked her. "I've only just come down, I 'll get you some tea shall I?"

"Goodness William, I'm not used to this. You take Ann and I will do my tea. You found everything you needed? She really meant had he found the 'gazunder', but felt too embarrassed to ask.

"Yes thank you. I didn't sleep well I'm afraid, such a lot we have to do."

Florence noted he'd said 'we' and not 'I'. She said nothing, but felt so comforted.

"I'll go to Belgrave, but first I must go down to Duns Lane to see what's happening there, then go to Earps', then to Belgrave, so I'll be gone for some time. Where do your parents live – the Dolphin isn't it? And the Ginns, they have a yard and stables a little further out on the other side of the road, that's right isn't it?"

"Yes William, I should come with you, I must. While you go to Duns Lane and Earps' I'll go and see if Annie Johnson will have Ann."

"If you want to. I'm sure you want to see your parents. I'll bring a carriage up from Duns with me."

"That would be wonderful, maybe I'll bring Ann with us, what do you think?"

"Would save you bothering the Johnsons. It is Saturday anyway. Remember I am at All Saints tomorrow."

"I'd forgotten, of course, it is Sunday tomorrow. Thank you so much for all you're doing for me. We will be ready at noon shall we?"

"Yes, no later, I must hurry now, I have a lot to do."

William arrived before midday, and helped Florence and Ann into the carriage.

"How long will it take? Is she a good horse?" Florence shouted. But it was noisy and William was facing away from her. He replied, but Florence couldn't hear, so she just leaned back on the buttoned velvet seat and wondered how her Grandpa coped; he was almost stone deaf. How did her grandmother manage?

She felt Ann change weight and looking down, saw she had gone to sleep. She needed to alter her position, as she was lying on the 'bump'. By the look of it, the bump would be a baby soon. She was worried about telling her parents. Although her mother knew her daughter's marriage wasn't good, it would still be a shock.

She hadn't had a minute to talk to William about what had happened at Earps'. She knew she still had to register Frank's death. So much to do. Thank heavens she had William helping her.

They were almost there, and Florence's stomach lurched; she couldn't tell if it was the baby or nerves. The carriage pulled up outside the Dolphin. Ann stirred and William came around and helped the two of them down, squeezing Florence.

"I'm with you, we can do it, come on" he said. They walked up the steps and went into the pub to find Florence's parents. They looked delighted to see her and Ann, but were perplexed at seeing William and not Frank.

"What a surprise! Ann, you are so far from home!" Then Kate saw the expression on her daughter's face. "My dear, what is the matter? Where is Frank?"

"Oh Mother, he has passed away! It was so sudden, he'd been in the stable mucking out Drambuie, then he walked up the yard to the house and Annie Johnson made him a cup of tea and he went to sleep in his winged chair, but when I went to look at him he'd gone! William here has been so kind, helping me sort everything out."

"Oh my dear! I know you weren't happy, you and Frank, but what a shock. Where is he now?"

William spoke up at this moment. "Well I haven't had a chance to tell Florence yet, but he is now at Duns Lane, not at Earps'. My men came and took him this morning. Mr Earp was not happy, but he let me collect him. I have a hearse, so I will take charge of the funeral for Florence, if she would like me to."

"You are a good friend to have, how would you have managed, Flo?"

"I can't imagine Father, I really can't. We still need to tell the Ginns, can I leave Ann with you, Father? Will you come with me Mother, please?"

"Of course I will, it isn't going to be easy but of course."

They crossed the road and walked up the hill until they came to the stables. Florence held her mother's gloved hand tightly until they were in the yard, where Mr Ginns saw them. Straight away he knew something was wrong from the expressions on their faces.

"What's wrong, is it Ann?"

"No, Mr Ginns, oh I'm so sorry! It's Frank, it's your son. He has passed away, Mr Ginns, yesterday. It was so sudden, he just went to sleep and died in his chair."

"Oh no, not Frank!" Mr Ginns turned white with shock. "What was it?"

"You know he fell up the stairs after the christening. The doctor came to see him and told him to go for tests at the infirmary. He said his colour made him think there was damage to his liver. He didn't go for the tests. He told he would drink much less, but it stayed the same." Florence knew she was talking too quickly but couldn't stop herself. "They think it was cirrhosis of the liver, but I'll go and see Doctor Angus next week to find out."

Breathless, Florence turned to Mr Ginns. "Shall we go with you to tell your wife or will you do it alone?"

Mr Ginns' eyes were full of tears.

"I'll tell her. Thank you." Feeling relieved, they went over the yard back to the Dolphin.

"I suppose he will want the carriage and Drambuie back, when he thinks about it" said Kate.

"Oh Mother, what can I do?"

"At least you didn't tell Mr Ginns what his son was really like."

"Things usually work out for the best. You have William by your side, don't you? He is a good man I think, I liked him when I first met him."

"We'll have a cup of tea and change Ann then we must go."

"I understand you have a lot to sort out, but you'll get through this Florence, you'll see."

"I know, Mother. But the truth is instead of feeling sorrow I'm feeling relieved. Is that wrong?"

"After the way he abused you, no it isn't wrong. He wanted a son, he never gave any time to Ann. I just hope this one's a boy."

CHAPTER SEVEN

It was dusk when they arrived home, and the temperature had dropped a few degrees. The evening sky was flecked with red; Florence hoped that meant it would be a good day tomorrow.

"I must bath Ann before she goes to bed, the air seems chilly now" she said.

"Shall I leave the horse and carriage here tonight?" replied William. "I'll take them back to Duns after I've been to church. Or on Monday."

"You can put your horse next to Drambuie, I'm sure he would like the company. I won't be long out of bed tonight, it's been a hard day and my back is aching."

"I'll go and sort Megan out in the stables, then what shall I do tonight?"

"Please stay in the spare room again tonight. I feel more confident than I did last night, but it is good to know you are not far away."

"It's Sunday tomorrow - you go and bath Ann." Looking at Florence, he saw how tired and pale she looked.

"I will, she will be in bed when you get back, and when we've eaten I shall go to bed too."

Florence put the water on to heat, then bathed Ann. She took her up to the cradle, which really was too small. She must get another, from Cank Street, she'd seen good cots in there. She wondered if the babies should share a room. Then she wondered how Ellen was; maybe her aching back reminded her of the labour she had with Ann.

William came in and washed. Florence said she was going to bed without supper, leaving him alone. She felt so wretched that she felt no guilt. She went to bed without even looking in on Ann.

As Florence lay in bed her backache seemed to come and go, and she realised they were contractions; she had to get help. When her next contraction was over she went to the back bedroom. William had just settled into bed.

"William, the baby is coming" she said. "Please fetch Annie!"

"Oh my Lord" he said, climbing out of bed and slipping on his shoes. "Let's get you back to bed."

The lamps were lit in Highcross Street, although it wasn't very late. William stayed with her during her next contraction, then hurried round to the Johnsons'. Annie was just going to bed.

"There is no use in asking Ellen to help, she is worse I hear" said Annie. "Will you be all right Walter?"

"You go Annie, it is all happening at 98, isn't it?"

The first thing they heard when they opened the door was the sound of two babies crying. One of course was Ann, but the other was a newborn, still tethered to Florence by the umbilical cord. Annie took a look at the little creature. It was a boy.

Florence had agreed with Frank that if the new baby was a boy they would name him after his father.

Annie had never had to cut a cord before, but she had seen Ellen do it several times. Once it was done she found some warm water from the kitchen. William had been in with Ann all the time. Annie called to him as she hurried to the kitchen for warm water. Before that she covered Florence, who was shivering now. Then she turned to the new baby and washed his face and his body, thinking how sad it was that his father had not lived to see his long-awaited son.

When little Frank was clean Annie gave him to Florence to cuddle and try to feed whilst she cleared up everything. "I need to change you and your sheets, Mrs Ginns" she said.

"Later Annie, let me rest for a while. Will you find the old drawer and make it up for Frank please, open the window and cover the mess on the bed? Then Mr Gutteridge can bring Ann in to see her brother."

"Yes Mrs Ginns, I know where the drawer is and I'll tell Mr Gutteridge as I go to get it."

William came in then, carrying a bleary-eyed Ann. "Look Ann, that's why your mother was so noisy it woke you" he said to her. "You were so happy he'd arrived, weren't you Flo? Can we see him? What have you called him?"

"We decided on Frank if it was a boy, so Frank it is."

Frank had a lot of dark hair, but his eyes were firmly closed. "All babies have blue eyes to begin with, I'm sure" said Florence.

"My John did when he was born, but they are changing now, I think they'll be brown in the end" said Annie. "Sorry to interrupt. The drawer is ready at the side of the bed."

"Florence, I am so glad it's a boy and that you are both healthy" said William. "Goodnight, my dear."

"Goodnight William."

Annie noted the spark of warmth that flew between them and smiled a little to herself. "It shouldn't take me long to clean the bed" she said.

"I'll sit on the chair while you do the bed" said Florence. "Will you put the sheets to soak in the coppers until Monday?"

"That's a good idea Mrs Ginns, I will. He's a lovely baby."

Annie soon had Florence back into bed with clean sheets. Frank had finally taken some milk from his mother and the house was calming down for the night.

CHAPTER EIGHT

On the Sunday morning, William went home for a change of clothes before he went to All Saints. Florence lay in bed talking to Frank and Ann and thinking how busy William would be tomorrow, registering both a death and a birth.

Annie came again to look after her until William returned. Florence was glad of the company.

"I hope both Walters can manage without you, I shall be glad when things settle down a bit, won't you?" said Florence.

"I'll be very glad, but you have a good deal to do. I hope you won't mind me saying this, but I am glad Mr Gutteridge is able to help you."

"So am I, Annie."

William came back after church and immediately went up to see Florence, who, having just fed Frank, was dozing in bed. Annie had taken Ann out; she was starting to walk at last.

"We have a lot to sort out next week" said William.

"I know, I'll do what I can."

"Tomorrow I'll go to Greyfriars and register Frank's death

and the birth of the little one. Then didn't you want a cot for Ann? I need to go to Duns Lane and see what's going on there, I'll have to leave George Salter in charge for a time. And we have the funeral to organise."

"Would it be easier if you brought some carriages and the hearse here, I wonder? And someone needs to go to Belgrave, with happy news this time. And I need to see a Mr Hooper, I think it is, at the bank fairly urgently. Who can go to Belgrave? I wish we had a telephone like Dr Angus."

"When things are sorted maybe we can get one, I think they will be very popular, just think!"

"We have so much to do, but it is much easier with you to help me dear" smiled Florence.

"Where did Frank want to be buried?"

"He bought a plot before the new cemetery on Welford Road was opened. His father bought one too, you know. You don't buy the land, you buy permission to be buried in it. But of course you would know that!"

"Frank told you that, didn't he? Most people think they own the piece of land. You must have talked about it. That makes things easier. Where did you marry?"

"Frank hadn't been a churchgoer, he only went when he was working. He wanted his service in the chapel at Welford Road, and he wanted me to do the same, which I won't."

"That makes it easy for me, I'll make the arrangements tomorrow."

"Shall we send telegrams to Belgrave?"

"Good idea, saying what?"

"Well… 'Frank junior 6lbs 12ozs arrived Saturday, all well. Florence'."

"I'll take it to the Post Office tomorrow morning. I know it's Sunday, but circumstances alter cases. I suggest we have bread and cheese to eat. I'll just go down and check Drambuie, then I'll get it for us."

"Thank you, William. If you can pass Frank to me I'll feed him while you're gone. Will you take Ann with you now? She can walk. I'm sure she'd like to see Drambuie."

"Of course I will, if Annie has brought her back. I'll take some bread down and show her how to feed him."

"I think she's a bit too young to do that, William, maybe when she's a bit older."

"Maybe you're right."

Annie had returned and was boiling an egg for Ann, who looked tired. So she would be in bed instead of seeing Drambuie. William went down to the stables and stood thinking it was all going so well with Florence, it was as if it was meant to be, it seemed too easy; it must be right. He gathered his thoughts and filled the hay bag up. He must write a list of things to do tomorrow, nothing could be done until Annie arrived at eight tomorrow morning.

Annie had changed Ann and put her to bed, then went in to see if little Frank needed changing; he did. When it was done, Annie said she would be back tomorrow.

"William has a lot to do tomorrow, I must get myself a new black dress as I'm now a widow" said Florence.

Monday morning found William up early. He'd written himself a list and he would begin at Duns and let one driver bring a carriage and pair round to number 98 while he would go and register Frank's death and the birth. Very strange that they had happened so close together, and Frank had never seen his son.

The registrar was incredulous. "I have never dealt with this before, the baby is to be Franks Ginns too! It beggars belief."

"The name was chosen by his parents long before he was born" said William.

"So you are?"

"Just a friend of the family."

William took the certificates, folded them neatly and put them into his wallet. He walked into the sunlight of Greyfriars and back to Highcross Street. There he went to the Post Office. He was surprised at its state of disrepair. He sent two telegrams to Belgrave, then turned his thoughts to the carriage and pair; had Michael delivered them all right?

Turning into number 98, he saw the carriage. He went to the stables to find that the two new horses had hay and straw and Michael had cleaned the tack.

William went up to the house and went up to see Florence.

"Hello my dear, how are you, how are things here?"

"The children have been good. How did you get on?"

"To begin with I went to Duns and had Michael bring a carriage and pair round. Maybe you heard. Then I went to see the registrar, who was amazed. He had never known such a thing before. I have the certificates in my wallet. Then I sent two telegrams to Belgrave. Then I came back to 98, saw Michael had done what I'd asked him to do, and here I am."

"I'll get up tomorrow. I need to buy some black clothes and a hat for the funeral. When will you be able to do it? We need to let people know."

"George has laid Frank out. I'll go to Welford Road tomorrow."

The gates arrived, and two men were asked to lay them under the newly-erected 'bridge' between 98 and 100. They were about eight feet high, made from wood. The top half was made from wooden bars, painted black, while the bottom was solid wood painted in a dun shade. The blacksmith had put hoops half way up each gate and sent two metal bars with hooks to be attached to the wall underneath the bridge so that the gates could be closed and secured at night. It would be Charlie's job to open them in the morning.

William hadn't forgotten that he needed to see Mr Hooper with Florence at the bank, but the funeral must come first. He went into the house to tell Florence about the gates. Ann rushed to him as soon as she saw him with her chubby arms outstretched, wanting him to pick her up, which he did without hesitation. It seemed quiet and dark in the sitting room, but then he realised that Florence was on the sofa feeding little Frank.

"I didn't see you, it's so bright out there and dark in here" he said. "Tomorrow I'll go to Duns and see what arrangements have been made, then I'll go with you, if you'd like me to choose something to wear at the funeral. Will Annie take care of Ann and Frank do you think?"

"I hope so, we will have to go just after I've fed Frank. Ann will be all right as long as we aren't too long."

William was out early and was back from Duns Lane about the same time as Annie. Florence had almost dressed and fed Frank; she would leave Annie to dress Ann while they went shopping.

Morgan Squires, a new shop in Leicester, was the first shop Florence wanted to investigate. Perhaps because it was too new, it didn't seem to have very much stock or choice, so they left with nothing. Florence decided they would go through the market to Morley's, which had more choice.

The first thing Florence thought she would do was to look at the dresses. She needed one which wasn't totally black, preferably a cheerful one, but she knew she couldn't have that. She looked through the rack of dresses. She chose a black one trimmed with white; that was as far as William thought she could go. It had many pin-tucks around the waist and she realised she had only just given birth; it was bigger than the last one she'd bought. Now she needed a hat, which she had seen downstairs. First she tried one with a black bow to wear under her chin. The hat began half way over her head with an inch-high arrangement of violets. It was rather funereal, they both thought later.

William was wandering around the shop whilst Florence was trying on hats when he saw something sparkle quite low down, under a counter. He asked the assistant to show it to him. It was a cape, studded with jet and made of fine Nottingham lace. It was perfect, so he bought it without a second thought. He went back to Florence carrying bags with a dress and present for her, deciding to give it to her when they were home. He could see she wanted to get home, so they paid and left, William carrying the bags.

As they were walking up High Street, William said, "We must send telegrams to Belgrave and tell them about the funeral."

"Yes, as soon as we get home" answered Florence.

As they neared number 98 they were pleased to see the closed gates, which looked strong and sturdy. Charlie was standing inside, looking a bit perplexed.

"Don't worry Charlie, you'll have to use the Front Office

door to get in in the morning, and open them about eight" said Florence smiling.

Charlie opened the gates and they went into the house.

"Annie, I hope we haven't been too long" said Florence. "It was my fault, we went to that new shop, Morgan Squires, but left empty-handed. We went back to Morley's, where I bought a dress, not too sombre - I'll show you when we've had a cup of tea. Where are the children?"

"I'll make the tea, Mrs Ginns. Frank's outside in the pram and Ann seemed tired so she is sleeping on your bed. I hope you don't mind, the cradle seems so small for her now. Did I do the right thing?"

"Of course you did."

Annie went to the kitchen. They sat down and Florence took the bag holding the dress and held it up. The hat would smarten it up, she thought.

"I thought you wanted a cape?" said William.

"I did, but we ran out of time, didn't we?"

"Look in that other bag."

She opened it to see the cape, made of fine black lace and studded with tiny pieces of Whitby jet. It would always remind her of Frank and now, not knowing of the past, William had changed bad to good. What a kind man he is, she thought.

William explained the funeral arrangements to Florence. He suggested that he should bring the hearse and two carriages up from Duns Lane and go from Highcross Street. They had to be at the chapel of Welford Road Cemetery at 10.30 on Thursday. It could be quite difficult getting up the hill and then turning sharp left into the cemetery, so they must just pray it wouldn't be a wet day. The burial would be in the best position in the cemetery, a much better position than the grave bought for James Cook later.

They would go to the Joiner's Arms for the wake. Frank had spent a lot of time and money in there when he was alive, so it seemed the right place. William suggested if that was all right he would go and send telegrams to both sets of parents, if Florence agreed. She wondered about flowers, but decided not to confuse things, so he went over to the Post Office to send them. She would have to think very carefully what she would write on the wreath cards. William suggested he should buy the wreaths from Gibbs, the florists which he'd used many times before. He told Florence he would bring her a choice of cards for her, but she decided only to sign his children's card. She didn't want to appear a hypocrite. Buying the hat and dress had been enough of a struggle; no more.

Everyone assembled at Highcross Street at about nine o'clock on the Thursday morning, even Florence's brother, who had really had little time for Frank; he knew how Frank had treated his sister, both from his sister and his mother. Florence later found out the real reason; he was emigrating to America, which upset her more than Frank's death.

The service was very short, as Frank would have wanted, and fortunately it wasn't raining. The committal didn't take long either. A few tears were shed, mainly by Frank's mother, and then it was back down the hill to the wake. Florence was so glad she didn't have to pretend any more, she was just sad about her brother's news. What a day to find out.

Ben Parker had laid on a good spread, though it was his wife, Alice, who had prepared it. Florence felt right in what she was wearing. The black of the cape showed the white through though it, so it was toned down. Some of the mourners knew and understood. Penny and Agnes came too. Annie Johnson was looking after the children at Friars Causeway with her grandson. Florence was glad when it was all over.

William hadn't wanted to be any more than the funeral director, but Florence was comforted to see him there, in his top hat and tails too, together with the feathers about the horses heads; they were said to frighten the Devil away, but at times she wanted to laugh, not cry. Then she remembered her brother's news, and her heart sank again.

William was waiting at number 98 when she arrived home, He had changed from his work clothes into a sombre suit.

"The worst is over, my dear" he said. "You must think of today as a beginning and move on, not as an end."

"I know the worst is over, it was worse than many will know. I thank you for your support; I don't know what I would have done without you."

Things settled down after the funeral and William said to Florence that he felt she too had settled down, but while he would try to call in each day they must live apart. This saddened Florence, as she had grown used to his support; he had said he would go with her to see Mr Hooper at the bank, which she must do now the funeral was over. The following evening was to be William's last evening in the spare room.

Annie came in to work a few days later and asked to speak to

Mrs Ginns. "Jack has a new job and we are to move to East Street" she said. "I would still like to work for you, but it won't be so handy as now."

"Oh Annie, when do you leave?"

"Two weeks on Friday. Will you still want me to work for you? Mother has said she will look after John until we meet new friends there. At the bottom of East Street they have just built a new place where you can buy large blocks of ice, to use in shops, fish shops and anywhere else to keep things cool. It has just opened."

"Where is he going to be working?"

"At Watkins on Gypsy Lane. The other piece of news is that Walter has had to call the doctor for Ellen, he says she will be gone by tomorrow. All change on Friars Causeway, it seems."

"That is terrible news. Of course I shall still want you to work here. Do tell Walter to see Mr Gutteridge when Ellen passes away, Annie please."

It was William who told Florence of Ellen's death when he called in to see her on his way home from Duns Lane. Florence remembered she had brought Ann into the world and felt sad for both Walters, young and old.

"It's all funerals at the moment isn't it? When is there going to be something happy?" said Florence.

"I really don't know, my dear. How about we go to see my parents in Belgrave on Sunday? We can take a carriage and take the children with us. It will be a change of scene for us."

"Would your parents want a mother and two babies foisted on them, do you think?"

"Mother especially would love to meet Ann and Frank, I have

told them both about them. They don't really live in Belgrave, that's why we never met. We have stables at the back – but you will see on Saturday."

"I shall look forward to meeting them."

Florence still missed having William staying in the back bedroom. She went to meet Mr Hooper at the bank, where he told Florence that, basically, there was no money left; Frank had used it all to buy drink. This was a huge shock to Florence, as she had not had a clue. She'd been led to believe by Frank that they would build an embalming room, a rest room and enlarge the kitchen. Now she was a single mother of two with no money at all.

William and Florence had discussed what Florence was going to do to help William, and they decided she would engrave the brass nameplates. William gave her the tools and some instruction and a green velvet cushion to tie the plates on while she engraved them.

It seemed the first should be that of Ellen Disley. She began sitting at the table, which she soon realised was the right height, and if Annie Johnson wasn't about to keep her eye on the children, she could shut the door to the kitchen, then know what they wanted or needed. William would collect it that evening. After two attempts, it looked right.

Florence kept thinking about what to do. Should she go back to her parents, or ride it out? Perhaps she should get a mortgage, all that talk about enlarging the kitchen and building an embalming room had been pie in the sky she now realised. Then, to make matters worse, Mr Ginns Senior arrived to fetch

Drambuie and the carriage, not concerned about what it would do to Florence. She felt so sad, so alone, so overwhelmed. What to do?

Then William arrived to collect the breast plate, and saw her anguished face.

"What's wrong Florence?" he asked.

"I need your help, everything has gone wrong. Mr Ginns been and taken the carriage and Drambuie, and I have no money."

"I have been thinking about your problems. First I think you, or we, should go back to see Mr Hooper and ask him for his advice. You were in shock when we were last there. See if you can take out a mortgage to help you get yourself out of the mess Frank has left. The other thing I've been thinking of is moving my Duns Lane business up here and paying you rent to keep the carriages and horses here. Please think about it."

"William, that would help me so much, the mortgage I mean. The rest I need to think about. There is Ellen's breast plate, what do you think? I had to try it twice." "That's fine, let's hope there will be many more to work on. You'll get quicker with every one you do, thank you for engraving it dear."

Sunday arrived and William came in his favourite carriage. it was the one they had taken to Belgrave last time.

" When we went to Belgrave before it was just me and a bump" she said. "A lot has changed so fast, hasn't it? And you never showed me your home, did you?"

"No I didn't. Have you had any more thoughts about what we talked about on Thursday? Because I have. Florence, I would like to ask you to marry me. At least you will know that I love you, and have since I first met you at All Saints. Now seems the right time to ask you. In fact I've been down to Mr Hyde's to choose this ring. Only if you say yes, of course."

"Oh William, yes, yes! I've loved you since that day too! So I am going from being Mrs Ginns to Mrs Gutteridge."

Florence Gutteridge, goodness! The children would stay as Ginns though, she thought. And just days before she had thought nothing was going her way.

They didn't have time to talk. William put the ring on, quite unceremoniously. He was more worried about getting Florence, Ann and little Frank aboard; Frank especially.

Finally they were ready. It was a dull day, with no promise of sun, which was a shame. Florence had taken off her first wedding ring and put it in her black leather handbag without a thought when William put on the new engagement ring. She felt both relief and joy. William was about the same age as Frank, and surely healthier.

There was a little excitement when they were going along Loughborough Road and were overtaken by a motor car, a black Rover. Even Ann looked at it in awe. There seemed to be more of them every week.

After about ten minutes William slowed down, into the back of a large house and stopped. He climbed down and rang the doorbell, twice. "It just lets them know it's family" he explained. "Let me take Frank and you can sort Ann out."

"What a beautiful house! I have been by it many times but never knew..."

Just then the door was opened by a man wearing glasses. It was Jabeus Gutteridge, William's father.

"William, what a pleasant surprise ! Who do you have with you?"

"Father, this is Mrs Ginns and her two children. This is Frank and that is Ann."

"Delighted to meet you, Mrs Ginns."

"Mr Gutteridge, please call me Florence" interposed Florence. Ann ran off down the gravel drive, delighted to feel the white stones crunch beneath her little shoes.

"Let's go in and see your mother, William" said Mr Gutteridge. "She has heard so much about the children."

They walked across a wide hall, floored with flagstones, into a large room where a lady was sitting on a settee. Florence knew it was Juliana, William's mother. Without speaking to her she immediately liked her, as she had his father.

"My dear, this is Mrs Florence Ginns" he said. "And her two children, Ann and Frank. At last you may meet the people I have told you so much about."

"Please call me Florence, Mrs Gutteridge" said Florence, wondering if William was going to tell them that she was to become a Gutteridge too. Jabeus found some pieces of wool, then sat down on the floor and began to play with Ann. Frank sat on William's knee.

"We have something more to tell you both" said William. "Florence and I are to be married; I proposed this morning before we left and she accepted. We have known each other since Ann was a newborn."

"You've kept that very quiet, although you did talk about Florence a lot, William."

"Maybe, it is more a woman's thing to think about than a man's, I suppose."

"Would you like to see my ring, Mrs. Gutteridge?" asked Florence. "It is so new I have hardly seen it myself!" The ring was a dark sapphire with small diamonds around it, and Florence thought it was beautiful.

"What a wonderful surprise! so there is to be another Mrs Gutteridge. But you are by the look of it, still in mourning."

"Yes Mother, but next summer..." said William. At that the dark clouds above decided to make their presence felt and large spots of rain began top lash the windows.

"Do you want to put your carriage in the stables for a while, William?" asked Jabeus.

William looked at Florence, "What do you want to do, dear?"

"I need to feed Frank really. Before anything else."

"If you'd like to go into the little room next door while Will sorts the carriage, I will make some tea." So the onset of rain made everyone busy.

Monday morning saw Florence so excited, for she could not wait to tell Annie. When she arrived she could see something good had happened to Florence, as she was full of smiles for a change.

"What has happened?" she asked.

"Mr Gutteridge asked me to marry him yesterday and I said yes. Look!" She held her left hand out to show Annie the ring.

"Mrs Ginns, I am so happy for you! You have not been very happy since I started here. Mr Gutteridge is a good man, I think."

"He has supported me since Mr Ginns died, as you know. He is a kind man, too. We went to see his parents yesterday afternoon and they are both good people, I liked them very much. William has told them all about us, and the children seemed to feel at home, which was lovely. Now I need to tell my family, my brother is off to America soon remember."

William was used to sending telegrams, Florence thought, but she decided to go to the Post Office herself and send it. We must get a telephone, she thought. She was sure William would feel the same.

William called in after work as normal. He was interested to hear that Florence had been to the Post Office and sent a telegram to her family. She reminded him that her brother was emigrating to America very soon and they must go over, and see him, maybe next week.

"Do you think it would be a good idea if we had a telephone, especially if we are going to run a business from Highcross Street?" she said. "Doctor Angus had one when I went to see him with Frank, though most of his advice fell on deaf ears. I shall be eternally grateful, dear."

"We shall have to consider that."

"I did tell you that Annie and Jack Johnson are moving to East Street, but Annie will still work for us, which made me think of the changes in Friars Causeway. When Ellen's funeral is over will you have a word with Walter and tell him we still need him to work for us, even though Mr Ginns set him to work?"

"I have already talked to Walter. He just needs this week, then he'll be back on Monday."

"Good."

Mr Hooper at the National Westminster Bank in St Martin's was high on their list of people to see. They arrived there just after the bank had opened. It was the biggest bank in Leicester and it had a very high domed ceiling, painted with figures from mythology. The building echoed, and Florence loved walking up the steps to go in as it made her feel special, important.

After they had waited for a few moments, Mr Hooper came out and showed them through to his office, which seemed small after the cavernous main bank.

"Mr Hooper, we are here to see if we may be able to get a mortgage" began William. "Mrs Ginns and I became engaged this weekend. I am moving my removal and funeral business from Duns Lane to a property owned by Florence and her recently deceased husband, Frank Ginns. I own three carriages and one hearse which we will move to Highcross Street, however a good deal of building work needs to be carried out. Mr Ginns had begun it, but, as you know, things have had to be stopped. If we could get a mortgage we could build what we need, couldn't we dear?"

"Yes, we really want to make it work. I was so shocked to find Mr Ginns has left me with nothing. I have two babies and really don't know what I would have done if it hadn't been for William."

"Mr Gutteridge and Mrs Ginns, thank you for talking to me. I do understand your predicament. How much were you hoping to borrow?"

"We were hoping to borrow one thousand five hundred pounds" said William.

Mr Hooper asked a few more questions, then said, "If you leave it with me and come back at the same time on Friday I will give you our answer."

They both thanked him and left the bank. The next job was to buy a cot for Ann; it was amazing how much she'd grown. Frank would then sleep in the new room over the gates.

The next day was Ellen's funeral. The service was at All Saints and the committal at Gilroes Cemetery. Florence decided she wouldn't go but would look after the various children; Annie had known her for longer than she had. So she stayed at home, though she would have liked to be there.

Before they knew it it was Friday, and again Annie was left with the children. Ann had slept her first night in the cot, fitfully as it turned out. Mr Hooper was waiting for them when they arrived, which William thought was a good sign, which it was; he told them they could have their mortgage. They were ecstatic. Now they could really build.

When they finally had time and the children were in bed, William and Florence sat down at the oval table in the sitting room.

"The first thing we must do is write a list of anything we think we want to do" said William.

"A telephone, a bigger Kitchen, an embalming room, a rest room, room to park the carriages, a roof over the yard perhaps" said Florence. "And get the upstairs toilet finished."

"I agree with you about the telephone. If we are to have a business here, it is I think the way forward."

They decided to enlarge the kitchen and build the embalming room and rest room first, and see how things went before they spent more money. William would get a quote from Jack Harrison; The work he'd done before was good enough but needed to be finished. Frank had left a debt which Mr Gutteridge paid so the work could continue. The kitchen - how wonderful it would be to have space! Once the toilet upstairs was finished then it would be the kitchen. As for the floor for the kitchen, Florence wanted it to be tiled like the front doorstep from Highcross Street, small, matt black and white tiles, how well they would go in the kitchen.

CHAPTER NINE

It was another six months before the builders finished. The new kitchen seemed vast, so much so that they decided to put a bath in there too, covered with a pinewood table top which you could bolt open if you were having a bath. The kitchen floor was as Florence had wanted and was looking even better than expected.

William had to wait four months for the roof over the yard to be finished, so the carriages had to stay in Duns Lane, except for his favourite and one horse called Quentin, which gave Old Walter something to do for now.

"I thought it was going too easily" said William.

"You went to see the man who owns the land on Great Central Street, what did he say?"

"Well, I offered him what we agreed, but it wasn't enough. We need to see Mr Hooper again, to see if we can borrow more. We will have to work really hard to repay it, but we really need the space for the carriages and cars in future, I think, the way things are going."

William could have asked his parents, but although they liked Florence they were concerned that he was saddling himself with a widow with two tiny children.

Although Annie had moved to East Street, she seemed happier and Johnny was soon to be walking. Florence wondered what she would do without her.

The christening took place before Christmas; the wedding would be the next event. They agreed to have only a small ceremony, but to book a photographer, as this was the new fashion. Like the telephone, wedding photographs would soon become very popular.

William's parents were becoming friendlier every time they met Florence and the children. There had been a big party for Francis before he left for Liverpool with his friend, Roger Ryan. They were both planning, eventually, to get to San Francisco. Mr Cambers had to comfort himself with the knowledge that maybe one day there would be an American branch of the Cambers family.

William went alone to see Mr Hooper.

"Good morning, Mr Hooper, I'm sorry I haven't made an appointment. We now have a telephone which, I hope, will make things easier for us all. The original mortgage has been virtually spent and everything is almost ready for business. However, whilst working at number 98 we realise we really need more room to park the carriages. I have been to see if we can buy some land from a Mr Surridge, but he wants more than we can afford, so I have come to see if we can extend the mortgage."

Mr Hooper smiled. "I'm not surprised to see you again, Mr Gutteridge. I have heard reports of what you have been doing. Shall we go into my office?"

"Of course."

"So you would like to borrow more money, what am I to set it against?"

"I own three carriages, one of which is a hearse, which I seem to be using more and more. I seem to be getting some of Earps' business, which seems a good portent, so perhaps I could set them as a guarantee."

"I am not surprised you need to enlarge your mortgage. Do you have any other security?"

"Not really. My parents have a business on Loughborough Road which is worth quite a lot of money, but I do not want them to become involved in this, to be honest."

"Can I ask you, with respect, why you don't want them to be involved?"

"Because Mrs Ginns and I want to do this independently. I hope you can appreciate that, Mr Hooper."

"You do know that the mortgage will take twenty-five years to pay off, don't you?"

"Yes, we know it is going to mean a lot of work, but at this time, as we are getting the business started, we both want to do with your help."

"I do understand. I'll give you a telephone call tomorrow afternoon after I have discussed it with my colleagues. What is your telephone number please?"

The following day Mr Hooper rang to say that the new mortgage had been approved and William told Florence the good news. "This seems so easy, Florence" he said. "I can go and see Mr Surridge and try to negotiate with him. He knows we need the land so he won't be let it go for nothing. You realise that, don't you?"

"I know that, but I know you will do your best dear."

"Right" he said, taking a deep breath. "I'll go and see if he's there."

Mr Surridge was in his office when William tracked him down. It was small, dark and musty smelling, and you had to climb up three rickety steps with grass growing between them and knock at a black door. Mr Surridge was about fifty and slightly balding. He opened the door, then went back to sit behind an old wooden desk with copious amounts of paper spread before him. He was surprised to see William so soon.

"Mr Gutteridge, I assume you have had time to see your financial advisor and you have come to tell me your news, very quickly it seems. Speeded up by the use of a telephone, I imagine."

"Quite so, Mr Surridge. We would like to buy the piece of land but not at the price you first spoke of. Some negotiations need to be made."

The negotiations took an hour. Then, when they had reached an agreement, Mr Surridge dropped in some new information which surprised William. He had another piece of land adjoining the premises which William already owned in Highcross Street. Would he be interested in buying that as well? Again they negotiated, and finally reached agreement. They shook hands and Mr Surridge said he would instruct his solicitor to set things moving.

Florence was washing Frank in the sink in the kitchen when William walked in through the back door. "Guess what I have done dear, I do hope you think I did the right thing. I feel I did, but it will involve you as much as myself. Mr Surridge has also sold us another piece of land. You know that old piece of ground that goes from opposite the sitting room window to Friars Causeway? There is nothing there but a small building which I think was a house standing at the corner of Highcross Street and Friars Causeway. We can expand that way too eventually. It was cheaper to buy two bits from him than one. I really hope you agree with me."

"Oh William, what have you done? Is there going to be any money from the mortgage left? We are going to have to work very hard now, aren't we?"

"Yes my love, we are. It will be hard for a time. I hope you don't think I have been wasting money, but it was too good to miss. You do still want to marry me, I hope?" The wedding was only three weeks away.

"Of course I still want to marry you. We have so much to do, but it's only going to be a small wedding isn't it? I'm glad. Your parents are coming. Shame Frances won't be here."

"I wonder where he is now? I would think he has arrived in America."

"I should think he will write soon. Oh, Walter came in while you were with Mr Surridge, and Quentin needs more food. Is he to get it or will you get it along with the Duns Lane horses? I told him you'd see him tomorrow."

"I will, we can't do any more until the solicitors have done their work. I think I will telephone Mr Hooper tomorrow and go to see David Goddard and tell him about the new acquisitions and ask him to act for us."

"I have been meaning to ask you, but you haven't been around much lately. Who is going to be your Best Man?"

"I have asked my brother, Harry. We haven't been over to Kirby Muxloe to see him and his wife for ages. Who are going to be your bridesmaids?"

"No bridesmaids dear, as I have been married before! I am asking Penny and Agnes to be my attendants. They won't be wearing bridesmaids' dresses, just similar ones to mine I think. I shall be glad to come out of mourning, from black to white!"

"It will be lovely to see you in a more colourful dress again."

"Yes, I will be more relieved than you can imagine."

Flowers were arranged in the church on the morning of the wedding, and Harry Gutteridge stayed with William on the Friday night in his flat on St. Nicholas Street. Florence's parents stayed with Florence at Highcross Street. The relations from Hathern must have left very early in the morning, and were glad that Highcross Street was their side of Leicester. Clara and her husband George were glad it was on a Saturday, as she was a headmistress and could not have attended on a weekday.

Penny and Agnes, the attendants, had come to Leicester the previous night and stayed with their parents. They arrived dressed in pretty pink dresses. Then Florence appeared, glad to be out of mourning, also wearing a pink dress, a little darker than theirs. Florence wasn't wearing a veil, but she managed to make an impression when she arrived downstairs.

When everyone was ready and the church clock chimed in the distance, Annie scooped the children up and rushed over to join the others in church. Florence's father took his daughter's arm and walked down to the church.

As she waited at the church door, Florence remembered the first time she had seen William; so much had happened since. She was going to walk down the aisle as Mrs Ginns and back as Mrs Gutteridge.

The service went well, made even better maybe because William was a Churchwarden. When everyone was back at number 98 they were surprised to see that a collection of chairs had been arranged by Charlie and the photographer. The bride and groom were asked to stand on chairs at the back and others collected around them. The children were asked to stand at the front, on the ground. Some of the guests were a little dubious, but they co-operated and all had their photograph taken. Then they went up the front stairs to the newly-built room where Frank usually slept. Annie had changed him, fed him and put him in the pram. In the room Alice Parker had laid out a buffet and Florence's mother had brought a wedding cake which she had made. There was wine and champagne.

Florence introduced William to her relations from Hathern, who she hadn't seen since her last wedding. Harry stood up and made a short speech and then asked his brother and his wife to cut the cake. A while after that, William told his new wife that they were going to Ireland for a week and Penny and Agnes were staying to help Annie with the children; it had all been organised weeks before the wedding.

"My goodness, who's paying for it?" asked Florence. She was concerned that they could not afford such extravagance.

"It is a present from my parents to us, my dear."

"What a lovely surprise. Can we go and thank them now? I will write to them after we've been. When do we leave? Where shall we stay?"

"I have all the information in an envelope which came from Thomas Cook's travel company to my old address last week. We can read it in bed tonight."

"I hope not!"

"I thought you were eager to know all about it!" He smiled. "We go tomorrow."

Florence took William's hand and they went over to see his parents and thanked them over and over.

"Who's looking after Duns Lane and here?" she asked.

"Well, George and Michael will be fine looking after Duns and Charlie and Walter will take care of this place. Don't worry dear, all you need to do is pack."

"This has been the happiest day of my life. I mean it, William."

The guests were beginning to leave, and Charlie had opened the gates. The relations from Hathern were the first to go, then Clara and George. Charlie and Walter began to tidy the chairs away, while upstairs Annie, Agnes and Penny all put on aprons and helped carry the buffet away so Frank could sleep in his normal room. When everything was washed and tidied away, Annie left Penny and Agnes to take over with Ann and Frank. She said goodnight to the newly-weds and wished them a wonderful week in Ireland, then left to go home.

Florence and William went upstairs with the children. Florence put Frank in his cradle, briefly thinking he was getting too big for it; they could organise another when they were home next week. Then William put his arm round Florence's shoulders and she turned to the children.

"Tonight is a special night" said Florence. "Now we can be together all the time, at night as well as during the day.

Tomorrow William is taking me on an holiday and Annie, Penny and Agnes are staying here to look after you. Someone will sleep in my room whilst we are away, so you will never be on your own." She knew they did not really understand.

William put Ann to bed and Florence put Frank in his cradle. Then the moment Florence had thought of, dreamed of, since meeting William in the church years before was finally here. There was to be no time to look at the itinerary for Ireland. Perhaps she should look on it as a mystery holiday.

The week away passed by very quickly. William kissed the Blarney Stone and was amazed at the Giant's Causeway and the green of the countryside. It did not rain once, which was just as well as Florence had packed very hurriedly the morning after their wedding, and as she hadn't had much sleep the night before she had forgotten her mackintosh.

Soon they were aboard the ship *Celtic Connection* and heading for home. Florence was longing to see her children again. William had said while they were away that he intended to treat Ann and Frank as his own and if they were lucky enough to have children themselves, he would treat them all equally.

Highcross Street didn't look the same as when they had left a week before. The gates were closed; William thought Charlie was still doing a good job. When they walked in they surprised Agnes, who was reading near the window.

"We are home" said Florence. "We have had a wonderful honeymoon. Ireland is lovely, the people are so friendly and it didn't rain once! But where are the children?"

"Oh Florence, how lovely to see you! Penny has taken Ann

to feed the ducks at Abbey Park. We didn't tell either of them you were coming home today. Frank is asleep upstairs. Would you like some tea? Penny made an apple cake yesterday, I'll bring you some of that too."

After the honeymoon it should have been a time to relax, but it proved to be a busy period. There was a garage to build, rest rooms, a wall and another toilet to be built, then horses to bring up from Duns Lane.

And then Florence found she was pregnant. Maybe the leprechauns had helped.

The baby was due at the end of August, so Florence could carry on with Annie Johnson's help up until the baby was born.

It was a boy, and they decided to call him Arthur along with all the surnames his mother had in the past, so he was christened Arthur Cambers Ginns Gutteridge, in All Saints church, where his mother and father had met several years before.

The rest rooms were soon completed. There were four of them, each identified by a letter. Since the hearse had been brought up business had improved a good deal, to Mr Earp's chagrin. Not a lot of love had been lost between him and William since the affair over Frank Ginns' funeral.

Annie was more than pleased with the new kitchen and envious of the new bath. She, Jack and John had to use a tin bath near the fire, all using the same water. By the time John had his bath the water was a little murky. The water first had to be boiled by the fire, then poured into the bath; no wonder baths were not taken very often. Annie really was envious of the newly-installed boiler.

The telephone was being used more and more. William was woken by it at all hours of the night to go out and make funeral arrangements, first going to Walter's to arranged for him to collect the body with the hearse. He was thinking it was time for them to buy a funeral car, now that they had a garage. He kept putting the decision off, until his father made his mind up for him by saying he wanted to buy him a Rolls. It proved to be the first of many.

Jabeus said, "I will think of it as an investment. You and Florence have set up mortgages and bought land. Your mother and I are proud of you. Luckily we are in a position where we can help a little. First you must learn to drive, of course."

"Oh Father, I have been thinking about getting a car but I'd decided to wait until we had more money. It would help the business to grow so much, Florence will be so pleased."

"I have had a look around. There aren't many places to buy them, but Castles seems to be offering the best prices. I know Mr Clutterbuck there. We can go and talk to him about it if you like."

"That would be wonderful, when can we go?"

"I won't be able to go until Thursday, would that suit you?"

"We have a funeral at Saffron Lane Cemetery in the morning, but the afternoon will be fine."

"Of course you will need a black one, that goes without saying."

I know that. Shall we meet at Castle's then? It's about half way isn't it? I will aim to be there at three o'clock."

"That's fine for me." With that, Jabeus left.

Florence wanted to go too. William said that it would be fine, as long as Annie would look after the children. Thursday arrived, and Annie brought John with her and was asked to answer the telephone if it rang. She wasn't sure she could manage this, and was relieved when they told her they weren't going to be very long.

They decided to walk to Castles; it was cloudy but it did not look as if it was going to rain. The nights were drawing in now, and Florence loathed the winter.

They arrived at Castles before Jabeus, so William asked for Mr Clutterbuck, who knew that William wanted to see a Rolls Royce; he had already talked to Mr Gutteridge in some detail about it the week before.

Then Jabeus arrived. "Florence, I'm glad you have come too" he said. "If you would like to follow me?"

They walked past a row of huge, shiny cars. Florence was amazed; she'd never seen so many cars, let alone Rolls Royces, before. Mr Clutterbuck stopped in front of the car Jabeus had in mind. It was black, of course, and had running boards with red leather seats. Florence sat in the back and was shocked to see two cut-glass decanters and glasses behind the driver's seat. She was stunned. What had she married into?

The carpet was plush, in a coffee colour, and the driver's area was red, matching the leather seats. Florence thought that if it was to be a working car the carpet would be better if it was similar all the way through; she would mention it later.

William got into the car, the first time he had ever sat behind a steering wheel. Now all had to do was learn to drive. They then all followed Mr Clutterbuck back to his office, where discussions about the car ensued. Florence interposed with her comments about the colour of the carpet. But time was marching on, so she gave her apologies and left to go to her children to relieve Annie. It had all taken longer than she'd thought.

"I'm so sorry Annie" she said on her return. "I have never seen so many shiny black motor cars and I sat in the back of a Rolls Royce. It was wonderful, and huge. What has happened here? Has the dreaded telephone rung? How are the children? How is John?"

"I'd left Jack a note telling him to come and fetch John if I wasn't home by six, and he came and took him about a quarter of an hour ago . I think motor cars are the way forward, Mrs Gutteridge, don't you?"

"Yes Annie, one day everyone will have a car, maybe ladies too. Most people don't go far from the town where they were born, but I think motor cars are going to bring a big change in years to come. Oh here's William. Hello dear, there was nothing to dislike was there? I was telling Annie all about it, but Annie, where are the children?"

"I have washed them and put them in their night clothes, and Arthur went into his cot like a lamb, he seemed very tired. I hope I did right. You will have to feed him soon, I think. Ann wanted to help me wash him, but he was too tired. I had the dirty clothes in the washing basket instead."

"Thank you Annie, what would we do without you?"

"Frank and Ann are playing with some bricks at the moment but they have become too quiet, shall I go and see what they are doing?"

"No Annie, I will go and bring them down here for a while" said William. "They will have forgotten what we look like. You go, and thank you."

Annie left as soon as William went upstairs with Ann and Frank. Florence looked up at the ceiling and closed her eyes. It had been a busy and unusual day and she wanted some peace and quiet, but she needed to talk to William about the car, too.

She was beginning to drift off to sleep, but she pulled herself back from the arms of Morpheus just as William walked in carrying Frank and holding Ann's hand.

"Say hello to your mother, both of you, please" he said. But they didn't want to; they both wanted her to hold them, kiss them and talk to them. William was forgotten.

"Shall I go and make us some tea and get milk for the children?" said William.

"That would be appreciated."

The children climbed over her, and she sat Frank on her knees while cuddling Ann. *"Roll along, covered wagon, roll along, to the tune of your wheels I hear a song,"* she sang, bouncing Frank faster and faster on her knees *"City ladies might be fine, but give me that girl of mine, roll along, covered wagon, roll along."*

At this point, to Frank's amazement and surprise, Florence split her legs and his weight fell through on her dress. Frank giggled and Ann screamed; she wanted a go too, it appeared.

William came in with the drinks, asking what all the noise had been about. Florence told him, so it was his turn with Ann this time, then Frank wanted another go.

"When we've finished our tea and you've drunk your milk then one more go each and then it's bedtime" she said.

As if by magic, a sound of crying came from above. "I'm needed upstairs" said Florence. "I'll feed Arthur, then he should sleep for the night."

William took the other two up to bed a few minutes later. Florence still hadn't talked about the new car, but it would be better with no distractions, she thought. Arthur was crying and took some time to pacify; all he wanted was his nappy changing and to be fed. After that had been done he seemed wide awake, so he was taken downstairs so that William could see him for a while when the other two were settled.

While William was happy to see Arthur, he would rather he'd been left in bed. He wanted to talk to Florence about the car. After a few minutes, William took the baby back to his cot and left him grizzling for a while, then he too slept. By this time William was getting comfortable in Frank Ginns' old armchair, which he had moulded himself into over the months.

"I wanted to talk to you about the new car" William began.

"So do I, I wanted to wait until the children were in bed."

"Me too, what did you think?"

"Oh William, the whole afternoon was wonderful! I have never seen so many cars in one place before, all shiny and new. And Mr Clutterbuck, what a strange name he has! He was interesting too, I loved his bow tie. The Rolls was perfect, apart from the carpet, which I told you about. I saw its price! Your parents must be very well off."

"Well my dear, Father has a good business in removals, and mother was a Scott, a well-known family in Leicester, so you must come to your own conclusions. But what do you think? About buying the car?"

"I think if your parents are offering to buy it for us it would be churlish not to accept, what an opportunity! When do we have to decide?"

"As soon as we can."

"Well, we agree then, good. All you need to do now is learn to drive. Where will you go to learn? Will Castles teach you? In our new car? They will have made a lot of money on the sale so I think the least they can do is teach you how to drive it!

"Mr Clutterbuck has it all in train, I am going to be taught next week. It shouldn't be too difficult. It will have to fit around funerals, of course."

"I'm glad."

Some weeks later the new Rolls, registration letters OX, was in the garage in Highcross Street. William had driven her from Castles in Churchgate; he'd had several lessons from Mr Carlisle and now felt able to drive. There was little traffic and no test, so he felt free as a bird.

The first thing he did was to take Florence to see his parents. It seemed to take no time at all, and Juliette and Jabeus were very impressed. Jabeus thought he might buy one for himself.

Some months later Florence found herself pregnant again.

"This is the last time" she said. "I'm not having any more babies, four will be enough. Two is the end, do you understand, William? It is all I have been doing for years. Enough is enough do you hear?"

"Yes dear, four will be enough I. Agree with you."

A fortnight later another boy was born, leaving Ann very outnumbered. They called him William after his father. Perhaps things would calm down now. Again William was christened in All Saints, as all his siblings had been. Reverend Swingler had retired and gone to live in Thurlaston. The new vicar, a Reverend

Ife, was a tall, dark-haired young man, newly married. He would fit into Highcross Street, Florence thought.

Highcross Street was changing; since they had demolished many streets full of terraced houses and moved the occupants to New Found Pool the congregation of All Saints had diminished. The cobbler's shop was still on the corner of a very narrow cut-through between the new Great Central Street and Highcross Street. The Co-Op was still open, and there was a wool shop where wool was sold in skeins; you had to get a friend to hold the skein while you wound a ball of wool yourself.

Old Walter was still living alone in Friars Causeway, except when Mick, his son, was on leave from the Merchant Navy. Walter had now moved up to the coffin shop, as he felt looking after the stables was a bit of a stop-gap provided by Mr Ginns. The coffin shop, with all its new machines, was better suited to him. The oldest piece of equipment was a frame used to build the coffins around. There was a long piece of metal in the middle, with which to make the width of the shoulders. If the corpse was larger than average a 'WFE' – Wide Foot End – was added to the order.

When the horses were brought up from Duns Lane, the drivers also moved. A "mess room" had been built at the bottom of the stairs that went up to the coffin shop. In the mess room the men changed into their business clothes, always black pinstriped trousers, smart white shirt black tails in the summer and a woollen coat in the winter, and always a black silk top hat. Black tie too of course.

There was a cooker, a kettle and in the middle of the room was a large square table. Nearby were the stables and at the bottom of the old yard then there was the new garage with the new Rolls Royce. Florence still couldn't believe it was theirs.

Michael and George were happy to be at number 98; maybe everything would settle down now. Walter had taken control of the coffin shop and Jack Warwick, a new recruit, was put in charge of the polishing shop. The horses were looked after by the driver; this included the carriage, tack and stables.

At the top of the yard was the house and gates to Highcross Street. Charlie, much to Florence's delight, had a new electric engraving machine, so no more doing it at the table. Again it was Jabeus who paid for it; Florence's life had been much enhanced by his generosity.

Every Sunday Florence took Ann and Frank to the small hall attached to All Saints to attend Sunday School. The school was run by Mr Laurence Jackson and his wife Faith (her name made it hard to choose hymns when they had married!) Arthur and young William were left with Annie Johnson, who always used a bike on a Sunday, having been to the early service at St. Saviours. William, being a churchwarden, had arrived earlier.

After an hour in Sunday school, the children having been very noisy, Mr Jackson rose to his feet, and a hushed silence fell. Mr Laurence was going to give the stamps out. The stamps were brightly coloured and depicted stories from the Bible. When each child had begun here, his parents had been shown a pale green booklet with spaces for stamps.

Having collected Ann and Frank, Florence saw Diana Harrison, whose son had done most of the building work at number 98. "Mrs Harrison, I saw you in church, it is so nice to see you again" said Florence. "How are you coping? It must have been a difficult time for you, I am sure Jack did his best for you. Are you still in Highcross Street? It sounds as if I'm being inquisitive but it's not really, I haven't seen you since John died. I so wanted to ask you for tea. Can you come on Tuesday afternoon about three, when Annie can look after the children? I have these two from my first marriage to Frank Ginns and I have two more now.

"Mrs Gutteridge, thank you, I would love to come over on Tuesday, but I can see you have your hands full now, perhaps it will be easier to talk on Tuesday."

"That would be lovely, I'll see you then." With that Florence steered the children towards home. Since the horses had been brought up from Duns, business had improved and they were now even making funeral arrangements for gypsies and fairground folk, who always paid, in cash, immediately. William talked to Florence and his father about buying another car, or maybe even a hearse. After a long discussion, bearing in mind the loans they still had, Mr Gutteridge said he would like them to get an accountant to look at their books. William knew just who to call, so he rang Mr Hooper and asked for a meeting in Highcross Street.

At the end of the following week, Mr Hooper said the business could afford a new car and how good it would be to have a fleet of shiny black Rolls Royces. They rang Arthur Gutteridge, who said exactly the same but told them they must 'grasp the nettle' and get rid of the horses and move on to cars, as he had done. He had bought a Rolls, too. No more shilly shallying. They could have an 'arrangement' with Juliana and himself, to be drawn up by a solicitor.

But before this could happen, tragedy struck; Juliana had a fatal heart attack. It was a total shock, as she was only forty-seven. Mr Hooper would be working on Juliana's will. Things were very different now. Most of the mortgages were paid off; the inheritance and a little more from William's father saw to that.

The funeral was in Belgrave Church and the men only attended. They went to the newly-opened cemetery on a hill the other side of Leicester called Gilroes for the interment. Building work was under way as they were going to build a crematorium. William decided to buy two prime plots near the crematorium. The headstone was to be of slate, with deep-cut lettering.

It took some time for the change to filter through. Maybe they could order a new car now, but Jabeus pre-empted him. "Now your mother is gone, I won't be needing such a car so you can have it and I will get something smaller" he said. "That would suit me, and you I expect."

When William told Florence, she almost cried with joy. Two Rolls Royces - goodness!

In 1914 the First World War broke out, the 'War to End All Wars' as it was called later. Many men went off to fight, and many were killed. William was considered to belong to a 'reserved profession' and didn't have to go and fight. Annie Johnson's husband Jack did have to go, and when he returned he was very much thinner and had a terrible cough; he'd been gassed (with mustard gas) in the trenches, though he never talked about it.

Ann started at All Saints school. She was quite shy and not very big for her age. It would not be long before Frank could begin there too. Their great aunt Claira was the headmistress, but they received no favours. Ann, who obviously couldn't read, was given a peg with a picture of a horse next to it on which to put her coat. In the afternoons beds were put out after lunch for the small children to have a rest. Some went into a deep sleep, but most just lay there quietly for 45 minutes. Then they were given Plasticine to make pretend loaves of bread and some other food to play with in the toy house.

Florence soon began to bond with the new baby. To prevent confusion they called him Little Billie. His brother and sister and Annie Johnson spoilt him a good deal. Now Frank and Billie were at school too, things were beginning to be easier for Florence and Annie. When Billie was standing, Annie took him to Mr Brown's, on Hinckley Road, to have his photograph taken, as she had Arthur, when he had been about the same age. It was an indulgence at the time, but then something happened which made that picture far more than a luxury.

When Billie was nearly five he came home from school one day and asked his mother for a penny. The little boy he shared a desk with had died, and he wanted the penny for some flowers for him. The boy had had diphtheria. It was very infectious, and not long after that Billie contracted it himself. He became very ill, and on December 17th 1919, he died.

Everyone was in a state of disbelief and shock. Ann, Frank and Arthur were in tears, along with Florence who blamed herself. Both she and William were comforted that Billie had been christened in the same font as his siblings.

It was decided that Michael Musters would conduct the funeral, Rev. Ife would take the service, then hold the interment at Gilroes Cemetery, in the same grave that had been bought for Frank Ginns. The interment was just before Christmas, and it was cold and windy. Ann and Frank were not at school. Annie came in every day and helped shoulder the burden. So much for things getting better.

When the day of the funeral came, having a telephone really helped. Mourners were either given places in the cars, or asked to get to Gilroes independently. The service was to be at 10.30 in All Saints, then up to Gilroes. Michael took control of everything. The hearse, which was new, was fully checked by Dan O'Shea, as were the two cars. George Slater and Denis Farley, a new man, could both drive. All the vehicles were washed, then sponge and leathered (which the drivers had to do every night any way). There was a six foot long by two foot square dark metal trough of cold water, from which the drivers filled buckets. The leathers were wrung dry by putting them through an old mangle with wooden rollers.

The day began with a blue sky, but it went unnoticed by Billie's parents. He had been such a gentle, happy boy. Florence was inconsolable and William was not far behind.

The children were left with Annie. It was thought the whole event would be too much for them, and for Florence. Charlie closed the gates and locked the door of the front office. A kind thought, William thought when he heard. Florence was a little uneasy thinking of her son sharing a grave with Frank. Most people had no idea what he had put her through, but she knew.

Charlie had opened the gates and the office. The cars came back, disgorged their passengers and all went in for something to eat and a warming cup of tea. Annie's cooking was improving, although some said her Yorkshire puddings would still be better left in Yorkshire! William and the men had whisky. The children were pleased to see their parents again.

Life seemed to settle down after the funeral and the business grew and grew. Florence began to work part-time in the office with Mr Cornish as the children got older.

There was some excitement when William returned from making funeral arrangements for a family of gypsies. The old lady lived in a caravan at the side of a country lane. It was winter, and dark. The first thing he saw was sparks flying from the road, and then he felt a thud. William got out of the car to discover that the car had run over the chain of a bolting shire horse, which stopped it in its tracks – a lucky accident. The gypsies were so grateful that they made tea and even offered William hedgehog pie. William accepted the tea but not the pie.

After the funeral the gypsies paid in cash. They also gave William a china cup and saucer. As the years went on, this seemed to be a custom, or maybe they had too much crockery!

A letter arrived from Francis in America. He had not heard of his nephew's death, but at least they now had an address. He and Roger had settled in Sacramento, and were still heading for San Francisco. This ruffled Florence a little but she soon calmed down. It was time she and William looked forward, not back.

"Florence, I quite understood what you said about not wanting any more children, but, circumstances alter cases" said William. "How do you feel now?"

They were lying in bed, and it was almost a year since Billie had died. They had never broached the subject before, as both had felt it too raw. But maybe now...

"Oh William, you know how awful it was, still is" she replied. "Yes I would like to try again, but no child can replace Billie, you know that, don't you? And I am getting to the age where I may find it harder to become pregnant."

"I know, but it will be fun trying, won't it?"

Eighteen months later Florence proved that she wasn't too old when she gave birth to a daughter. William and Florence were surprised, as they had assumed it would be a boy again. At least she would be her own person, and not be expected to step into the shoes of her late brother.

The parents had to scramble for a name. William said he wanted her to be called Florence, but Florence said "No, it's an old-fashioned name and it is too long. I like the name Mary."

"Well we can have her christened Florence Mary and she can decide when she's older, can't she?"

Ann was so pleased to have a sister, or at least a half-sister. Now there was a girl and a boy from each marriage. Florence once again decided four children were enough. Maybe now she could, with Annie's help, get back to the office.

The business was getting bigger and bigger. Florence worked on stonework mainly, liaising between the family. The most popular stonemason they had was Stan Bailey.

All the children were now at school, and even Mary was about to leave All Saints. Ann, being a girl, wasn't expected to go to work, however. Frank decided he wanted to become a funeral director, like his stepfather.

Now all the horses and carriages had gone. There was a bit of a furore when William first decided to only use a motorised hearse. What would repel the Devil if the horses and there feathered headdresses were no more? It was even reported in the *Leicester Mail and Mercury*. But William cared not, life had to move on. There were now two Rolls Royce hearses and Rolls Royce cars, so that two funerals could be put on simultaneously. William said jokingly, "people are dying to ride in our Rolls Royce."

By this time there were about twenty people employed by Ginns & Gutteridge, all men except for Florence. The embalmer was now Roger Black; they always wondered whether it really was his surname.

When Arthur's schooldays came to an end, he thought he too would like to be a funeral director. He was his father's son, and liked people. He was kind and caring. He wanted to help people get through a tough time in their lives, and he wanted to drive a Rolls Royce, apart from anything else! He told his parents, "I really want to be a good undertaker. I know you had a bit of trouble getting hold of Roger, where is he from? Not local is he?"

"No, he is from Lutterworth, not too far away" said William. "I was talking to him this morning in the embalming room. He was telling me he had taken an exam and now has a very impressive certificate and is a MBIE, a Member of the British Institute of Embalmers. I would like to do that. What do you think? And learn to drive."

"You've only just left school, hurry a bit slower, Arthur" said his mother. "You've obviously been giving it some thought and it would be good to have our own embalmer. Your mother and I are very pleased you have given it some thought. I always thought you had a brain in your head. Do you remember the incident at the Elephant and Castle?"

Florence had obviously forgotten all about it, so he carried on, though aiming his conversation towards Florence, rather than Arthur.

"Several years ago we needed two new black Belgian horses. I'd bought them before from a man in London, at the Elephant and Castle. It was the school holidays and Arthur asked if he could go with me. I said yes if his brothers and sister didn't mind, as he'd never been to London, so we went and caught the train down to Liverpool Street. We went to look at the horses, decided to buy them and looked for Arthur. He was nowhere to be seen, but there was no need to panic. He had some money in his pocket and a mouth in his head, so I knew he'd be home soon. Do you remember? He was home before me!"

"They weren't the horses that would try to dance when they heard music were they?"

"Yes they must have come from a circus, I think, not very good for funerals though, were they?"

"Have you noticed Ann seems to be more eager to go over to Mrs Cashuba's than she did?"

"I'm not surprised. I went by the other day when I was on the hearse. You know Mrs Cashuba died. Earps' had the job, I know. Well, her sister sold the shop to a Mr and Mrs Cox. Perhaps a boy comes into it somewhere, you'll have to find out, Florence."

Florence was more concerned about her elder son, Frank. He'd been out with a lot of girls in Leicester over the years, but he had been going out with one girl, Winnie Poole, for longer than most.

POSTSCRIPT

Some time later, after several visits to number 98, Frank and Winnie arranged to marry, in December 1931. Ann, in the meantime, had become very involved with the younger of two brothers, Horace, and they became married just after Frank. So only Arthur and Mary remained at 98. When Ann and Horace married, William and Florence bought them a house in Leicester, on 220 Welford Road; cows and sheep used to be driven to the Cattle Market at the bottom of the hill. Frank was given a house at 48 Scraptoft Lane with quite a big garden. He had five children in all, so it was well used. Ann and Horace had one daughter, Julia Mary.

One year Arthur went to Jersey on holiday with friends. It was a choppy crossing and Arthur helped a young lady who was very seasick. Her name was May Smith and she was from Oldbury, Birmingham. They married on 21st September 1938, at All Saints in Leicester.

May had previously been working in the offices of Chance Brothers, who made the lenses for lighthouses all over the world.

They also made glass plates. May's father Ernest worked there too, as did her elder brother Walter. Her younger brother, Albert, worked at Spear and Jackson. May's mother, Ann Tyler, was from Bishops Itchington, near Royal Leamington Spa.

When May married she'd already moved into Highcross Street and taken over the stonework from Florence, who was ready to retire, as was William.

After several weekends driving and looking around Leicester, William and Florence found a newly-built house further up Welford Rd from Ann and Horace, number 537.

When the Second World War broke out in 1939 it changed many things. Arthur was called up and joined the Army; the Tank Corps. Mary drove for the Air Force, while Frank stayed with his father, running the business. The war was making some differences to the number of funerals; there were slightly fewer of them, but there was also less choice of drivers.

Mary met an officer with the wonderful name of Douglas Rex Alexander Michael. She too was given a house, and they had one daughter, Elizabeth Ann Scott Michael, known to the family as Scotty.

After the war things changed again. William retired, moving to live with Florence on Welford Road and taking his first car with him. William and Florence were happy there until one day William was trying to lift his lawnmower from the boot of OX when he had a heart attack and died. This happened on May 5th 1949, and he was 69. It was a year since Susan had been born.

May liked to live in the hustle and bustle of Highcross Street, but she wouldn't see a corpse. She soon found out she was pregnant, and her daughter Susan was born on Florence's birthday, 17th April 1948, in a private hospital, the Fielding Johnson Hospital on Regents Road, Leicester. She was christened at All Saints Church and she too remained an only child.

Susan went to several private schools, then to Charles Keene Tech, then on to Loughborough Art College, then to secretarial college. After that she went to work with a friend, Jenny Cummins, as a mother's help in Marseille. She returned six months later, immediately joining the hostesses at the Leicester Post House, where she stayed for many years, leaving as a training officer. By then she had married Paul Hadfield, one of the chefs.

Paul and Su (as she liked to be called) married on May 11th 1974 at St. Denys church, Evington, and lived for about a year in a cottage in Woodhouse Eaves before moving to a house in Stoneygate, Leicester.

In 1976, Su found she was pregnant. She then discovered the neighbours had German measles. Su too caught the disease and they decided to have the baby terminated; it should have born on 4th January 1977. Luckily, by then, Su was pregnant again and Cassie Ann was born on 29th July 1977.

On 4th May 1979, the day Margaret Thatcher became Prime Minister, the nurses told Su that she was in Labour, and the Labour Party was losing! James Cambers Gutteridge Hadfield was born safely after a caesarian. Cassie and James both went to a Montessori School and then on to St John's school, where James was discovered to be dyslexic, so he went to a prep school which specialised in dyslexic boys. The headmaster, Mr Harrild, suggested he should go to Abbotsholme School in Derbyshire as a boarder. There James achieved a gold Duke of Edinburgh Award and several GCEs.

Cassie went to a local Catholic school, although she was Church of England, then went to live with Carol and Steve. She went on to catering college and university in Bournemouth, boarding in various lodgings. After taking her degree she travelled around the world, courtesy of her mother, who had done the same for James. When she returned she worked at Donald Russell, meat suppliers, later working as Events Coordinator at the Grosvenor House Hotel, Park Lane, in London, where she worked until leaving to have a daughter, Bethany May Greenwood. Bethany was born on 26th January 2010, exactly 100 years after her great grandma, Edith May Gutteridge (maiden name Smith). She was followed by a brother, who was named William.

THE END

CPSIA information can be obtained
at www.ICGtesting.com
Printed in the USA
LVHW041626170820
663417LV00011B/1705